DRAGONS AND BULLS
Profitable Investment Strategies for
Trading Stocks and Commodities

DRAGONS AND BULLS
Profitable Investment Strategies for Trading Stocks and Commodities

Stanley Kroll

ADDISON-WESLEY PUBLISHING COMPANY

Singapore • Tokyo • Seoul • Taipei • Hong Kong • Reading, Massachusetts
Menlo Park, California • New York • Don Mills, Ontario • Wokingham, England
Amsterdam • Bonn • Sydney • Madrid • San Juan • Milan • Paris

Production Coordinator: Salwah Saaban
Cover design by Daniel Chia of Xie Design, Singapore
Text design by Lesley Stewart, UK
Typeset by Times Graphics, Singapore
Printed by Longman Singapore

First printed in 1994

Library of Congress Cataloging-in-Publication Data

Kroll, Stanley.
    Dragons and bulls : profitable investment strategies for trading
stocks and commodities / Stanley Kroll.
        p.   cm.
    Includes bibliographical references and index.
    ISBN 0-201-42084-8
    1. Investments.   2. Stock-exchange.   3. Commodity exchanges.
I. Title.
HG4521.K748   1994
332.63'2--dc20   94-29648
                                                                       CIP

To Joyce
you are
'the wind beneath my wings'

Foreword

Stanley Kroll is a 'master' in financial trading and strategy. *Dragons and Bulls: Profitable Investment Strategies for Trading Stocks and Commodities* consolidates his depth and insight, gained during his 34 years on Wall Street. For individuals who want to take a leadership role in global markets, this book is useful for both analytical and operational purposes.

Dragons and Bulls offers focus against a contemporary and critical business landscape. I have prepared a translation for investors in China, where information on investing and speculating are limited.

Stanley Kroll started his career in 1960, on New York's Wall Street. During his 34 years of Wall Street trading, he accumulated a phenomenal amount of experience and wealth. He left the highly competitive Wall Street arena a millionaire and started travelling around the world. During this five-year sabbatical, Mr. Kroll enhanced his studies on economics, finance and investment strategies. He has written five books: *Dragons and Bulls: Profitable Investment Strategies for Trading Stocks and Commodities* is his sixth work.

In 1993, Mr. Kroll relocated to Hong Kong, where he now resides, and is managing director of his own financial consulting firm. He concentrates on managed futures trading, financial and commodity hedging, risk control and investment strategies.

Commodity futures and equity trading have just started in China. Compared with the 200-year history of Wall Street, we have a long way to go, especially as most Chinese lack experience in investing, speculating and risk management. In this book, Mr Kroll shares his decades of investment experience, and distinguishes himself with his own trading methods and strategies.

This is indeed a unique and valuable book for all investors and speculators, whether amateurs or professionals.

TIAN YUAN, PhD
Chairman and CEO
China International Futures Co., Ltd.
(CIFCO)
Beijing, 4 August 1994

Preface

For many years, I've wanted to write a book dealing with the strategy of trading both stocks and commodities, but for a variety of reasons, I never got around to doing it. However, upon relocating to Hong Kong in 1993, I felt that the time was right, and I set to work on it in earnest. It's unfortunate that so much of current thinking attempts to separate the strategy of trading stocks from that of futures, and most people think of the two markets as being worlds apart. In actuality, that is not the case.

Many experienced traders have come to the realization that speculative trading in both stocks and commodities have a great deal in common, notwithstanding many of the logistics being different. But, the basic tenets of sound trading strategy, of risk control and of the need for total discipline are common to both. The principal difference between the two markets is one of **leverage**, or **gearing**. Futures traders commonly trade on as little as 5% of the market value, while stock traders must generally put down 50%. It is the leverage that principally differentiates the two. If futures traders had to put down 50% of the contract value and stock traders just 5%, the situation would be completely reversed. Commodity trading would be considered conservative and sedate, while stock trading would be deemed risky and speculative.

This book acknowledges the vast difference in the gearing between the two markets. The strategies, tactics and risk control elements of both markets; those areas where they differ and those where they are similar, are discussed. It will become evident that the similarities are far more significant than the differences and that being skilled in one market can definitely be a big asset when trading in the other.

It should be noted that generally the discussion is principally about trend following, that is, trading in the direction of the predominant trend. For example, **buying on weakness into support** is a preferred way to trade, but only within the context of a major uptrending market. If the trend is down, even if buying into support, there is still likely to be losses. The same applies for selling short against an uptrending market.

Advice on the size of the position to trade is a little difficult. It is a bit like asking, 'how big is big?' If trading against the trend, and sitting with losses, even one contract seems excessive. On the other hand, if trading with the predominant trend, with the market moving generally in your favour, even a larger position can feel comfortable. However, to be more specific, in trading stocks, it is recommended that you do not use more than, say, 35% of your capital to margin positions; and for futures, not more than 25%. Furthermore, it is a good idea to diversify into about ten markets, so that a miscalculation or a mishap in one market can be cushioned by the performance of the overall portfolio. Dividing the amount you have available for margin by ten (more, for a big account) different markets, gives an indication of how big a position to take.

And finally, no discussion of strategy, in any field, can be complete without some mention of 'Murphy's Law.' This isn't really a law, of course, but an approach to events that, simply stated means, 'whatever can go wrong, will.' So, whenever you are careless about forgetting to enter your **protective stops**, or putting on too big a position in terms of a well balanced account even though 'it looks' *so good* on the chart, you are likely to become reacquainted with 'Murphy's Law.' Remember the old saying, 'whether the pot hits the kettle, or the kettle hits the pot, it's likely to turn out bad for the kettle.' Well, the same reasoning applies to speculation; carelessness and ineptitude are rarely rewarded by profits and favourably moving markets.

Here is a final word before you embark on this book. Readers are invited to write to me, care of the publisher, about any aspect of this book they would like to discuss further. I will respond to the best of my ability and time availability.

Contents

Foreword		vii
Preface		ix
Chapter 1	Introduction: The Man They Called J.L.	1
Chapter 2	The Importance of An Investment Strategy	5
Chapter 3	Winners and Losers	11
Chapter 4	Technical versus Fundamental Analysis	17
Chapter 5	The Art of War, by Sun Tzu (circa 2300 BC) and The Art of Trading Success (circa AD 1994)	25
Chapter 6	That's the Way You Want to Bet	31
Chapter 7	Those That Know Don't Tell; Those That Tell Don't Know	37
Chapter 8	Why There is No Such Thing as a 'Bad' Market	41
Chapter 9	Perception versus Reality	45
Chapter 10	Risk Control and Discipline: Keys to Success	51
Chapter 11	Long-term versus Short-term Trading	55
Chapter 12	Buy the Strength; Sell the Weakness	63
Chapter 13	Larry Hite: The Billion Dollar Fund Manager	69
Chapter 14	Creating and Using a Technical Trading System	73
Chapter 15	Trading Systems. Kroll's Suggested Method	79
Chapter 16	The Intricacies of Order Entry Procedures	83
Chapter 17	Epilogue: Kroll Market Strategy for Consistent Profits	91
Chapter 18	Postscript: Investment Opportunities in China and Hong Kong for the 1990s	95
Epilogue to Chapter 18		101
Appendix		103
Index		137

Acknowledgements

I would like to express my sincere appreciation to:

Knight-Ridder Financial Publishing, and Gerald A. Becker, Publisher, for permission to reprint materials from their very fine publications.

Dow-Jones Telerate, and David Fung, General Manager of Northeast Asia, for permission to reprint charts from their excellent Telerate system.

Edward Dobson, President of Traders Press, Inc., for permission to reprint portions of their edition of Reminiscences of a Stock Operator, by Edwin Lefebvre.

Salwah Saaban, Production Co-ordinator, Vivien Crump, Editor and to the staff of Addison-Wesley Singapore, for their months of dedicated assistance.

Tian Yuan, Chairman and CEO, and Wang Xinzheng, Executive Vice-President of China International Futures Company Inc., (CIFCO), Beijing, for their co-operation and assistance.

Reuters for permission to reprint a page of the News Service contained in Chapter 18.

1 Introduction: The Man They Called J. L.

As the plump aluminium bird curved westward toward Fort Lauderdale, Florida, the luminescent colour delineation between the Gulf Stream and the Atlantic Ocean was strong and clear. I slumped back in my seat while the jet began its final approach, reflecting on the main reason for my Florida fishing trip this Christmas holiday. I felt a compelling fellowship for a man they called J. L., and I was here because he used to come here.

I could picture him in his heyday back in the 1920s; tall, trim and intense, seated by the window of the speeding New York to Florida passenger express. Anticipating days of fishing and fellowship, relaxation and contemplation, and most important, a respite, albeit brief, from his heroic battles in the Wall Street and Chicago arenas. This was Jesse Lauriston Livermore.

Throughout this century, scores of brilliant or lucky market operators have had the heady and envious sensation of closing a position with a million-plus-dollar profit. I, too, on a few occasions, have had the good fortune to be included in this exclusive group. But Livermore was in a class of his own. For the sheer scope and magnitude of his gutsy operations, for the disciplined and calculating way in which he bought and sold, for the lonely and detached hand that he invariably played, he has never been surpassed by any other lone operator.

Jesse Livermore was born in Shrewsbury, Massachusetts, USA, on 26 July 1877, the only child of a poor farming couples. At the age of 14, he left home for a job, earning US$3.00 per week as a board marker at a Boston brokerage office. From this modest start, and through several years of apprenticeship, trading just small stock positions at various **bucket shops** along the East Coast, this quiet and dedicated young man became one of the most feared and admired market operators of the early part of this century. Other Wall Street operators nicknamed him, 'The Boy Plunger.'

Livermore's universe was price fluctuations, both stock and commodity, and his obsession, the accurate analysis and projection of these prices. Edward J. Dies, one of the great financial commentators of this era observed that, 'should Livermore be shorn of every dollar, given a small brokerage credit, and locked in a room with tickers and phones, he would re-emerge with a new fourtune.'

From my earliest Wall Street days, starting in 1959, Livermore was my hero. And, as I began developing my own expertise in price analysis and trading, he became my coach and mentor-in-absentia. Like many investors, I've been influenced by his tactics, his strategies and his market philosophy.

'There is only one side of the market, and it is not the bull side or the bear side,' he wrote in his book, *Reminiscences of a Stock Operator*, 'but the right side.' That basic philosophy is indelibly etched in my mind, and I revert to it every time I read some lofty or tedious market analysis excessively focused on theoretical hype rather than practical market analysis and strategy. Like most traders, I frequently face the decision of which positions to hold and which to close out. And here, Livermore provides excellent, clear-cut counsel through a commentary describing his own mistakes:

> 'I did precisely the wrong thing. The cotton showed me a loss and I kept it. The wheat showed me a profit and I sold it out. Of all the speculative blunders, there are few greater than trying to average a losing game. Always close out what shows you a loss and keep what shows you a profit.'

However, Livermore's most significant legacy to investors concerns an overall strategy regarding investment objectives. It is particularly relevant during these times when traders are becoming increasingly dependent on powerful personal computers and advanced software. Even relatively inexperienced traders are swinging in and out of sizeable positions on the basis of **tick-by-tick** and **on-line short-term chart presentations.** Pay heed to this piece of Livermore wisdom:

> 'After spending many years on Wall Street, and after making and losing millions of dollars, I want to tell you this. It never was my thinking that made the big money for me. It was my sitting. Got that? My sitting tight. It is no trick at all to be right on the market. You always find lots of early bulls in bull markets and lots of early bears in bear markets. I have known many men who were right at exactly the right time, and began buying or selling when prices were at the very level which should have made the greatest profit. And, their experience invariably

matched mine. That is, they made no real money out of it. Men who can both be right and sit tight are uncommon. I found it one of the hardest things to learn. But it is only after a market operator has firmly grasped this that he can make big money. It is literally true that millions come easier to a trader after he knows how to trade, than hundreds did in the days of his ignorance.'

Here is what Livermore said about losing money:

'Losing money is the least of my troubles. A loss never bothers me after I take it. But being wrong — not taking the loss — that is what does the damage to the pocket-book and to the soul.'

Regrettably, my Florida fishing trip was much too short, and about a week later, I was back to the freezing weather in New York. While waiting for the big fish to bite, I thought a lot about Livermore and his Florida fishing trips, about his trading strategy and his considerable market wisdom. And while his catch was undoubtedly more bountiful than my own modest bunch of kingfish, I enjoyed one advantage he couldn't possibly have had: I was able to study and enjoy his books.

* * * * * * * *

I composed the above words some years ago, but they are as timely today as the day they were written. They would have been relevant 50 and even 100 years ago, just as they will be 50 and even 100 years in the future. In 1849, Alphonse Karr said, 'The more things change, the more they remain the same.' That certainly applies to Livermore's investment strategies and tactics.

Jesse Livermore was probably the most dynamic and successful lone-wolf speculator and investment strategist of this century, and possibly of all time. Although he died in 1941, his influence on succeeding generations of stock and commodity traders has been enormous. I count myself as one of his disciples, having read and re-read his writings countless times. And, upon arriving in Asia, I was astounded to find how many stock and commodity speculators here feel the same about this investment legend.

About ten years ago, I had in mind to write a book about Livermore, using first-hand recollections from people who had known him and had worked with him in Wall Street in the 1920s and 1930s. I advertised in financial newspapers and magazines, seeking people with personal experiences of Livermore and his operations, but unfortunately, I was too late. I could not find anyone with such personal, first-hand knowledge. This was a big disappointment, but my own Wall Street career was active and busy, and I soon drifted away from this project into more constructive pursuits. However, I never fully discarded this Livermore project and, over the intervening years, I continued to study his writings and develop my own investment strategies with the assistance of Livermore's considerable wisdom and experience.

Gradually, an idea developed. If I couldn't write a new and relevant book about Livermore, why not write one with him? Write a book with a person who retired permanently over 50 years ago? A colleague suggested that the strain of over 30 years of 'trench warfare' may have been too much for me; unless of course, I had some new theories on the subject of mortality. Well, I had no such creative theories on mortality. What I had, however, was the realization that Livermore's tactics and strategies, although some of the best ever developed and enunciated for financial markets, may have become, over the years, a bit dowdy and 'tattered around the edges.' Perhaps they could stand to be updated and modernized, to be re-interpreted for a whole new generation of stock, commodity and options investors throughout the world; people who had grown up with fast personal computers, powerful software and **on-line tick data** which could be transmitted by satellite to the farthest corners of the globe with lightning fast speed? Developments and facilities Livermore could not even have dreamed about.

Traders in the 1990s and approaching the 21st century, analyse markets and enter orders in literally dozens of languages, while Livermore used only English and, quite likely, had never even heard a word spoken in any other language. To maximize usefulness, Livermore's teachings would have to be re-interpreted and modernized for scores of dynamic and active traders who had never heard a word in Livermore's 19th century New England dialect; and combine with my own relevant strategies.

As a matter of fact, I am sitting at my trading desk now, in Hong Kong, some 12,000 miles from Wall Street. It is here that I continue to ply my chosen profession, analysing and trading markets, alongside a myriad of financial operators who ply a similar trade in dozens of languages and dialects other than English. Thanks to modern satellite communications, I can 'fill' market orders in the same split-second interval that it took to fill similar orders from my desk in New York. But, there is one inconvenience which, unfortunately, can't be overcome with modern technology. Being located on the other side of the globe Hong Kong is hours ahead of New York time, so in order to trade the New York and Chicago markets a late start – around 8 pm working through to the small hours of the morning is the order of the day. However, there are of course many compensations for an American living in Asia, that easily overcome the modest inconvenience of working 'the night shift.'

2 The Importance of An Investment Strategy

Back in 1967, I received the following letter, part of it read:

'A New York friend sent me your World Sugar Market Letter of October 17, which I found interesting and subsequently quite profitable. The quotation from Jesse Livermore reminded me of my late and lamented father, who when I was a boy I asked how he made money on the futures market, his answer was, "You have to be bold and you have to be right." I then said, "What if you are bold and wrong?" and he said, "Then you go down with the ship."

His father did just that, unfortunately.

The ongoing dialogue with stock and commodity speculators has been an enjoyable and rewarding aspect of my career, and through diverse contacts, spanning a period exceeding 30 years, one recurring theme seems to surface. Even the least successful traders occasionally experience the big profits that are in the market – elusive and tough to capture – but there. And, if the considerable hazards of the big wipe-out can be avoided it is possible to take home large profits. But the question is how to avoid the financial disaster, the big wipe-out, that is all too common in the world of the serious financial speculator? Or, as expressed more poignantly in the above, letter, how to avoid 'going down with the ship?'

Ever since people got together and bartered stone tablets, tools, or just something to eat or to wear, there have been winners and losers in the trading game. Yet, despite the obvious profit potential and **high leverage**, most speculators, including many professionals, end up losers. Aside from the small number of professional operators, who **scalp in large volume** and pay only negligible commissions or clearing fees, the traders who make the big money on a consistent basis

5

are the longer-term position traders. They tend to be trend followers. I have been fortunate to have been on the right side of some big positions and big profits, some of them held for as long as eight or ten months and, as related later, one actually held **long** for five years.

The necessity of a first class, viable strategy is part of success in most fields of endeavour. It is no less relevant in financial speculation than it is in marathon running, tournament tennis, chess competition or corporate take-overs. The common denominator lies in the fact that success, or victory, involves both technical as well as strategic considerations. With so many players nowadays equally qualified in the technical aspects of their trade or profession, the thing that will distinguish the winner from the almost-winner is the consistent and disciplined application of first class strategy and viable tactics.

The correct utilization of good strategy is especially crucial in stock and commodity speculation. The basic rules are commonly known, but consider those traders who have never experienced a winning year regardless of how long they've been at it. Unfortunately, it's a relatively high percentage of speculators. Yet, they have surely heard, and can probably recite verbatim, some of those tried and tested maxims: 'the trend is your friend,' 'cut your losses and let your profits run,' 'the first loss is the cheapest loss,' and so on. Here is winning strategy in its most basic form, and probably all traders know them from memory. But, while consistent winners share a single-minded adherence to these basic winning strategies, consistent losers, on the other hand, are just as purposeful in their avoidance and violation of the strategies.

2.1 Basic Strategies

In summarizing the strategies and tactics you need to avoid the big wipe-out and to stand proudly in the 'winners' circle,' the following constitutes the essence of a basic strategy:

1. Participate only in those markets which are trending strongly or which are in the process of developing into a major trending formation. Identify the major ongoing trend of each market and take positions only in the direction of this dominant trend, or stand aside (see Figures 2.1 and 2.2).

2. Assuming that you are trading in the direction of the trend, initiate your position either on a significant breakout (such as a **gap opening on high volume**) from the previous or **sideways trend**, or on a **measured reaction** from the ongoing major trend.

    (a) In a major downtrend: sell on minor trend rallies into **overhead resistance** or against a strong down trendline, or on a

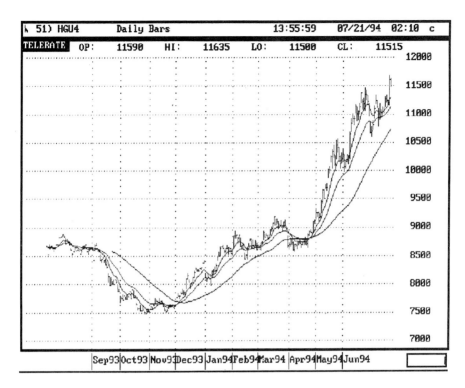

| ▶ 51) HGU4 | Daily Bars | | | | 13:55:59 | 07/21/94 | 02:10 c |
| TELERATE | OP: 11590 | HI: 11635 | LO: 11500 | | CL: 11515 | | |

Figure 2.1 *An Uptrending Market.* Commencing December of 1993, SEPTEMBER COPPER broke out on the upside. An uptrending market is typically characterized by a succession of higher highs and higher lows. Traders should not be anxious to sell their long positions and revert to short because bull markets generally go higher than most traders anticipate. The market, and your technical indicators, will "tell" you when the top has been seen.

    45% to 55% rally (or the third to fifth day of the rally) from the **recent reaction bottom**.

(b) In a major uptrend: buy on minor trend reactions into support or against a strong up trendline, or on a 45% to 55% reaction (or the third to fifth day of the reaction) from the recent rally high. In this regard, it is imperative to note that, if you misread or choose to ignore the trend of the market, and are buying against an **entrenched bear market** or selling against an **entrenched bull market**, you are likely to **spill lots of red ink**, and feel pretty silly, as well.

3. Your with-the-trend position could result in a big favourable move, so you should try to remain aboard for the ride. By premising that every with-the-trend position could result in the big move, you will be

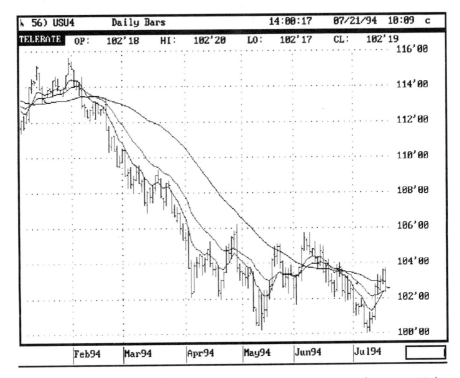

56) USU4	Daily Bars	14:00:17	07/21/94	10:09 c

TELERATE   OP: 102'18   HI: 102'20   LO: 102'17   CL: 102'19

Figure 2.2 *A Downtrending Market.* Commencing early February 1994, SEPTEMBER U.S. BONDS broke out on the downside, continuing down till late-April, when the trend changed to a broad sideways direction. A downtrending market is typically characterized by a succession of lower highs and lower lows. These bear markets generally continue lower than most traders anticipate; the market, and your technical indicators, will "tell" you when the top has been seen.

encouraged to resist the many temptations to trade for the minor swings, or to **scalp against-the-trend trades**.

4. Once the position is going your way and the favourable trend has been confirmed by your technical analysis, you can add to the position (**pyramid**) under specific conditions, as noted in Chapters 11 and 15.

5. Maintain your position until you are **stopped out**, and your trend analysis indicates that the trend has reversed. At that point, if you have been attentive to the market, you should be positioned for the newly formed trend.

In Chapters 11 and 15, the specific and detailed tactics of exiting a position will be discussed. However, if you have liquidated a position, and subsequent market action indicates that the major ongoing trend is still intact and that you have liquidated prematurely, get back on board. But, do it carefully and objectively, again initiating with-the-trend positions as discussed elsewhere in this book, notably in Chapters 11 and 15.

6. But, what if the market moves adversely, not with you as it's 'supposed' to? First of all, how will you know if it's a position gone sour? If you can't work it out, the daily equity run will 'tell' you in no uncertain terms. As a rule of thumb, you should probably not risk more than 40% of margin on a stock trade, or 70% on a futures trade.

Dickson Watts, a famous turn-of-the-century commodity speculator once said, 'run quickly or not at all.' He may have had a deep bankroll, or been enough of a masochist to include the, 'or not at all' part. My advise is to heed his words, minus the 'or not at all.'

And finally, while a consistent, viable strategy is clearly the main-stay of successful speculation, three additional traits are required: discipline, discipline and discipline.

The balance of this book is devoted to presenting and proving the above theses. I can patently attest, from personal (and painful) experience, that whenever I was careless or foolish enough to stray from these tenets, I lost money. On the other hand, it should come as no surprise that I generally made money when operating according to the strategies and tactics set forth here, for these are universal guidelines.

3 Winners and Losers

Someone once said, 'The best way to make a small fortune in financial speculation is to start with a large fortune.' It is unfortunate, but this cynical quote is very true, because the vast majority of active speculators, whether in stocks, currency, futures, **options** or **derivatives** end up losing money. Let us examine why this is so, and what we can do to position ourselves within the small, but winning minority.

In his memoirs, written in 1829, Bourriene recounts an incident in which Napoleon was asked which troops he considered the best. 'Those which are victorious, madame,' replied the emperor. I was reminded of this incident while perusing some notes on the subject of winners and losers in the investment arena. *The Wall Street Journal* of 10 January 1983, printed a survey of 20 senior commodity specialists and their best investment bets for the first half of 1983. Three points were given to a first choice, two points to a second choice and one point was given to a third choice. The ratings were totalled up and the results were extremely enlightening.

- Buy copper   18   points
- Buy gold   16   points
- Buy foreign currencies   15   points
- Buy stock indexes   14.5   points
- Buy cattle   11   points
- Buy silver   7.5   points

Some observations bear further consideration. First and most obvious, all recommendations were on the buy side. Not suprisingly, this proved a mistake since, of the top six selections, only two of them, stock indexes and copper, advanced during the six-month period. Of the remaining four selections, gold and foreign currencies were down, and cattle and silver just managed a sideways move. And, while all selections were biased to the **long side**, the few serious bull markets for that year, corn, soybeans, cocoa, cotton and sugar, were totally overlooked by the experts. It is noteworthy that copper appears so consistently on the list. Buy copper was also the second top selection in the previous survey (second half of 1982) and was the first selection in the first half of 1982 survey. The actual price action of copper, as well as the **composite decision** was mediocre at best during this year-and-a-half period. The copper market barely managed a broad sideways move for the entire period: down during most of 1982 and up during the first half of 1983.

The point of this exercise is to demonstrate how difficult it is, even for experienced experts, to predict the course of futures prices a mere six months ahead. The dismal record of these professionals should encourage serious speculators to note that the experts are frequently wrong and that a good technical approach to investment and timing, coupled with sound money management and a focus on trend following rather than trend predicting, are really the recommended ways to operate for optimum success.

There is a similar experience in the stock market between predictions of experts and a random selection of stocks. *The Wall Street Journal* conducts an ongoing competition, every six months, between two groups of 'analysts': firstly a panel of expert analysts and brokers and secondly the 'Dart Throwers,' a group of *The Wall Street Journal* staffers who randomly throw darts at the journal price page, and 'select' whichever stocks are hit. One would think that the 'professional experts' would consistently beat the 'dart throwers,' and by a very wide margin. But, that just hasn't been the case. Over a period of several years, the 'experts' have been ahead of the 'dart throwers'; but only by a narrow margin, at best.

Accordingly, a thoughtful student of financial markets should ask the question: why are the experts so often wrong and why do so many traders lose money at speculation? The answers may be circuitous and are often difficult to pin down. However, it may be constructive to reflect on what I call, the 'speculators' laments.'

With the exception of my 1975 to 1980 sabbatical, I have spent most of the past 34 years in a quiet, secluded office, either in Wall Street, upstate New York or aboard a large motor yacht, with trading monitor, phones, technical studies and other accoutrements. Consistently, my principal focus has been trying to make big profits on my favourable positions and to avoid taking big losses on my adverse ones. I have invariably played a lone hand, and very much by choice, having learned the benefits of operating independently early on as a Merrill Lynch account executive in New York in the 1960s. The lesson that I learned was this: it is not constructive to share trading ideas and market opinions with others, regardless of their opinions or presumed expertise. The universal truth on Wall Street is: 'Those that know don't tell; those that tell don't know.'

Over the ensuing years, I've occasionally had the opportunity to lecture or teach courses on speculation. My presentations have generally focused on market strategy, tactics and money management, rather than on specific market tips on what and where to buy or sell. Perhaps the most memorable of these events was a series of trading seminars I conducted in New York, Chicago, Miami, Los Angeles and Dallas on successive weekends. Attendees ranged in age from 19 to 86, with several husband and wife and father and son teams among the participants. The level of experience ranged from total neophyte all the way to experienced professional trader. In the course of the sessions, I managed to ask a lot of questions and the responses were particularly enlightening.

I discovered a surprising commonality of experiences among the several hundred attendees. And what I refer to as their 'speculators' laments' really weren't all that different between the novices and the experienced professionals, although the professionals were understandably reluctant to admit to them. Perhaps the frustration most common to all was: 'I watch while the market moves in the direction of my analysis, and finally when I enter a position, prices abruptly reverse and move in the opposite direction.' It should be consoling to know that all traders feel the same frustration at one time or another. It is, however, primarily a consequence of poor timing and tactics, rather than a 'plot' by other traders to gain the upper hand in the market.

A corollary to this situation is the following: 'I invariably find myself buying on strength near the top of every rally and selling on weakness near every bottom.' In fact, the accumulations of poorly timed buy or sell orders by speculators who tend to buy when everyone else is buying, or to sell when everyone else is selling, are what makes tops and bottoms, at least on a short-term basis.

The results of such careless and poorly timed trading is predictable— big losses and small profits. Do these quotations sound familiar?

'I told my broker to buy ABC, but he talked me out of it.'
(Translation: the speaker may have been thinking about buying ABC but didn't; and, predictably, the market advance.)
Naturally, the broker gets blamed for missing the trade.

'My broker called and advised me to buy XYZ. I wasn't keen on the idea, but he talked me into it.' (Translation: the speaker bought XYZ and it declined shortly after the trade.) Once again, the broker gets blamed for the losing trade.

If these quotations don't sound familiar, either you have just started trading, or you have a very short memory! These universal experiences express a quite universal phenomenon: that is, we invariably find a convenient way to rationalize our miscalculations and poor trades. I would like to suggest a viable antidote to this 'losers' mentality.'

Analyse your markets and lay out your strategy and tactical moves in advance, and in privacy. Don't ask anyone's advice, and that includes **brokerage advisories**, tips and even well-intentioned market gossip. And, don't offer your advice to anyone else. You shouldn't care if Shearson is buying ABC or if Salomon is selling XYZ. You should stick to your objective analysis and market projection based on whichever method or technique has proven viable for you; and you should revise that strategy only on the basis of pragmatic and objective technical evidence. Such evidence could be a signal from your chart analysis, your computer system or from the margin department, which reminds you that your position has moved adversely and that your account has become undermargined.

In short, if you make money in your trading, stand up and accept the accolades and the financial rewards. But if you lose money, you alone should accept the responsibility. You must have confidence to trade in the market, because the most serious 'loss' of all is the 'loss' of confidence in your ability to trade independently and successfully. If you don't have that confidence, you probably shouldn't be making any trades, except to close out adverse positions to limit your loss exposure.

The list of speculators' laments goes on, but they all seem generally related to carelessness or poor trade timing, misjudgement of the market trend, ignorance of the basic tenets of sound strategy, or lack of self-confidence and discipline. Serious introspection suggests this thesis: a sound strategy, viable tactics and good money management, and consistent risk control are even more important to overall success than a good technical or charting method.

Finally, no discussion of winners and losers can be complete without an examination of the 'desire to win' versus the 'fear of losing.' This is rarely discussed, but an understanding of this logic is essential for successful investment operations. A letter that I received from an investor in Australia focuses on the elusive pursuit of trading profits:

> 'My paper trading has always been far superior to my real time trading. In analysing why this is so, I am convinced that the answer lies in the simple truth of which is stronger — the desire to win or the fear of losing.'

> 'In paper trading, there is only the desire to win. In real time trading, there is principally the fear of losing.'

Isn't this the universal experience? Every one of us has been impressed at how much better our **paper portfolios** have performed versus our **real time portfolios.** The same could be said for the 'model portfolios' touted by brokerage firms and financial newsletters. Their hypothetical results invariably out-perform their real time results.

One of the reasons underlying this excessive preoccupation with the fear of losing is that the speculator often overtrades, both in terms of the size of the position as well as the turnover activity of the account. It is essential that the trader control and overcome these urges to overtrade or over position. My general rule is to utilize a maximum of one-third (for futures and currencies) or one-half (for securities) of the account capital to actually margin positions, with the balance of funds held in an interest-bearing reserve. Patience and discipline are necessary, since, on-balance, profits can only accrue to the operator who under-stands, and utilizes, accurate trade timing, albeit on a more modest scale, in favour of the more active trader whose tactics and trade timing are careless or innacurate.

Over the years, I have received scores of letters from speculators who have reported consecutive years of profitable results from using viable long-term computer trading systems, either of their own design or one bought commercially. The recurring theme in these letters is the necessity of following the system and its accompanying strategy precisely, in an objective and disciplined manner. These experiences can be a source of inspiration to those investors who find the pursuit of consistent profits, within a risk-controlled environment, an elusive objective. Chapters 14 and 15 are devoted to the use of computerized trading systems.

4 Technical versus Fundamental Analysis

First of all, some definitions: **technical analysis** is based on the actual behaviour of the market, as expressed by price, volume and size of the **short interest** (for securities trading) and **open interest** (for futures). The technician relies on the action of the market, through the use of charts and technical indicators, to help determine when to buy, to sell or to stand aside. **Fundamental analysis** is based on an analysis of the economic factors underlying the stock or commodity. It seeks to determine the basic causes of price change, and to evaluate whether a stock or a commodity is overpriced, underpriced or fairly priced, as rooted in economic factors such as earnings, dividends, price-earnings and other pertinent ratios, plus various balance sheet items (for securities); and production or crop size, carry over from the previous year, demand in the coming year and competitive supply (for commodities).

The best way to introduce this important subject is with a story — a true one.

My friend, Tony, who was one of the major floor brokers on the New York Mercantile Exchange, and I were sailing on the waters of Long Island Sound, New York. It was a hot, windless summer afternoon and we had been drifting along for half an hour, waiting for the anticipated two o'clock southerly wind to pick up and send us scurrying down Long Island Sound for an exhilarating afternoon of sailing. Neither of us was an avid conversationalist and we had exhausted our normal topics, which is probably why we got involved in the conversation I am about to relate.

Now, all my friends know my cardinal rule, that I never want to hear anyone's market opinion, nor do I care to give my own. But here we were, all of a sudden, talking about the heating oil market. Actually *we* weren't talking; it was Tony talking and me listening.

17

'I'll give you some very confidential information,' he said, 'but you must promise not to tell anyone.' 'Look,' I replied, 'I'm not interested in your tip, so please keep it to yourself.' I thought that would discourage him.

Wrong. It didn't take him more than a minute to recover from that mild rebuke, and he started again. 'Be serious,' he said. 'I'll let you in on it, but don't tell anyone that I tipped you.'

He was really determined, I thought; it must be something really special. And it sure was. 'Sheikh Yamani will shortly announce that the Saudis will double their oil production.' A long pause ensued. 'So what,' was the best I could respond. But Tony was persistent. '*So what?* Is that all you can say? Don't you realize the significance of this news? When the oil minister of the world's leading oil producer is about to announce that he will be doubling production, the market is sure to drop by US$20.00, maybe even US$30.00 over night. There's a fortune to be made here, and I've just dropped it in your lap. Besides, all the big floor traders have gone heavily short.'

I have heard all I cared to hear. Besides, who wanted to have this nonsense ruin what would soon be a great afternoon of sailing? 'Look,' I retorted, 'I don't know very much about the Saudis or their oil minister, or about oil production and its effect on heating oil prices. And I certainly don't know, nor do I care, about the "big boys" and what they do, or don't do in the market.' (Actually, I had heard so many 'big boys' stories through the years, that I was totally immune to them.)

'What I do know, though, is that this market is now heading sideways, but with a bullish bias, and in my opinion, it looks like it wants to break out on the upside and turn into a roaring bull market. So, can we please talk about something else, now?' Well I finally prevailed, although I had never seen this unflappable professional trader look so stunned. But my gambit rescued the day, and the balance of the afternoon turned out just fine.

The afternoon's conversation was very much on my mind that evening and, upon returning home, I wasted no time setting out my charts and technical studies for a careful re-examination of the heating oil market. Perhaps there was something in this scenario that I had overlooked or misinterpreted, and a careful double-check seemed like a good idea under the circumstances.

It was mid-July 1985, and the heating oil market had been locked within a tight trading range, between 70.00 and 73.00, basis the February 1986 future. Although the majority of traders were heavily short, some of the objective computer systems had already signalled to cover shorts and go long on 10 July, and I was just waiting for a close of over 74.000 – and the strong market action 'told me' that this breakout was likely to be imminent – to turn me full bore onto the long side, with the expectation of a major upwards move in the offing. Let the 'big boys' and their hapless followers exchange tips and gossip regarding Minister Yamani's anticipated announcement and its possible effect on the market. As far as I was concerned, I was anticipating a bull market, period!

Yamani either would, or would not, make the announcement; and even if he did, the bearish news was probably already been discounted in the market price. And the announcement, if there was to be one, would in my opinion, be the final ray of hope for the trapped bears prior to their being massacred by the strong and rampaging bulls. In short, my technical studies 'told me' that we were, once again, about to see the classic 'bear trap' in action. Discretion being the better part of valour, I opted to sit out this bear tip from the safety and serenity of my long position in February heating oil.

This was fortunate for me because, following a few more weeks of sideways price action, during which time the 'big boys' and their followers had ample time to get further committed on the short side, the market on Friday 26 July closed strong, just below 74.00 for February. That did it! The trap had been sprung on the unfortunate bears, and following one last gasp brief price reaction, the market commenced an impressive rally that ultimately carried some 16.00 cents, equal to US$6,700 per contract (see Figure 4.1).

What was even more amazing was the fact that Sheikh Yamani did, in fact, announce that he would be doubling oil production (Tony was at least right about that part of the tip) and predicted a sharp drop in prices. The market, however, is the ultimate authority, and was not impressed with this bearish tip. In its frantic race towards higher levels, it barely stumbled over the oil minister's 'epic' announcement. This must have shocked the intrepid and greatly pained shorts who, in the end, lost tens of millions of dollars due to their blind acceptance of a bear tip in a bull market.

There is a very clear-cut lesson to this story: beware of tipsters and other financial gossips bearing free market information or well-intentioned advice. And when the fundamental and the technical conclusions are at odds, you disregard sound, objective technical conclusions, or hang on to anti-trend market positions, at extreme peril. At all times, it is necessary to focus on an objective analysis of market trends and high volume breakouts from existing trends. Successful operators have trained themselves to ignore, and admittedly that's not easy, the hysteria and sounds of alarm that accompany the plethora of supposedly informed market pronouncements and tips.

Hong Kong has some of the canniest and most experienced traders anywhere in Asia. The Hang Seng Index futures provide excellent

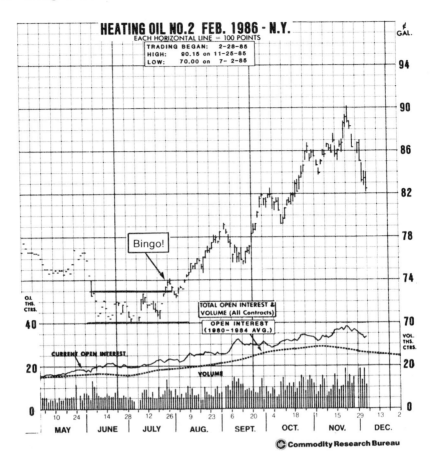

Figure 4.1 *February 1986 Heating Oil.* During June and July 1985, the market was locked within a tight trading range between 70.00 and 73.00. Despite major short positions on the part of many floor traders anticipating a bearish announcement from the Saudi oil minister, the market broke out on the upside on July 26, commencing a major bull move to the 90.00 level. This resulted in losses of many millions of dollars to the big guys and their hapless followers, who had been caught in the classic bear trap that they had so often engineered in the past. Their mistake? Following a bear tip in a bull market.

trading opportunities and action for speculators. Yet, throughout the three years, from 1991 through 1993, during a period of generally rising stock prices from a world class bull market, where prices rose from approximately 3,000 to over 12,000 (see Figure 4.2), traders continuously probed the short side of this stunning bull market. Every time there was some bearish-sounding news in the press, every time some commentator or interviewee delivered a bearish pronouncement, and especially when any British official talked about Sino-British

Figure 4.2 Long-term weekly chart of the HANG SENG INDEX, for the period July 1990 to July 1994. Note the impressive bull market lasting four years, during this period.

disharmony, the market suffered a serious bout of 'bear attack.' In fact, during late 1993, when the Hang Seng was undergoing its most violent and steep upwards move, I watched in amazement as a large office full of traders and account executives peered intently at a small TV monitor listening to a speech by Governor Chris Patten while the market was open. During the course of the speech, every time the Governor mentioned any aspect of Sino-British problems at the nego-tiating table, a flood of long liquidation and new short selling engulfed the market. Traders were apparently willing to totally overlook the ongoing trend of the market, which was clearly one way; up.

In fact, over the course of several months of an upward trending market, I heard dozens of pronouncements from brokers and traders that they were selling the Hang Seng for a number of diverse reasons.

- The market looked overpriced
- The market was due for a big correction
- They had received a bear tip that prices were about to turn down
- The principal reason for the rising prices had been massive buying by a big New York investment house which would shortly reverse to short and take the market down again.

In reality, the market was in a clear-cut and distinct uptrend and there was no viable, objective reason to play it short.

A large body of speculators had succumbed to a combination of undisciplined wishful thinking and a desire to be short in the market (they had liquidated long positions prematurely because prices were 'too high,' so they would now prove their acumen by getting aboard the short side). The great quantity of 'red ink' that accompanied these short positions was additional evidence, as if traders needed such additional proof, that trying to **pick off tops or bottoms**, against a strongly entrenched bull market trend is invariably dangerous to one's financial health and well-being.

The absolute need for a disciplined and objective approach to speculation, whether it be in stocks, commoditites or currencies, is a recurring theme of this book. We have all had the experience of relaxing our vigilance, of ignoring the real technical condition and direction of a market, which is generally clear if we are willing to see it. And, the results are uniformly predictable; unsuccessful trading and a string of consistent losses. Unfortunately hope versus fear, impatience, greed and, above all, a lack of discipline, are the major impediments to successful operations.

By way of an example; in the summer of 1984, the Chicago grain markets were in the process of breaking down from broad sideways trends into clear-cut downtrends. Most of the reliable long-term trend following computer trading systems had turned down, as had most objective chart techniques. This was confirmed, as though further confirmation was required, when the Commodity Research Bureau (CRB) grains futures index broke down through the 230.00 level (see Figure 4.3). Yet, the reality of this developing bear trend, so strongly entrenched that it persisted for two more years, was generally obscured by a steady barrage of bullish stories and articles in the business press about poor US growing weather and its damage to crops, unprecedented Soviet grain shortages which would lead to huge purchases of world grains and reduced Canadian crops. So, one has to ask, why were the grain markets sliding into a tenacious downtrend that was to last nearly two years?

A parallel situation was experienced in the metals markets commencing around mid-1984. Most of the market projections, economic analyses and brokerage advisories had predicted improving prices and had clearly recommended the long side of the metals markets. Long side indeed! And, here again, the CRB precious metals index tells the same story (see Figure 4.4). Prices poised on the brink of yet another downleg, soon to be confirmed by actual market action, during the relentless bear markets of the early 1980s.

Digesting such a steady stream of bullish pronouncements could hardly fail to give one a bullish bias. However, an objective and pragmatic review of the technical factors clearly showed that we were

CRB GRAINS FUTURES INDEX (1967=100)

© Commodity Research Bureau

Figure 4.3 *CRB Grains Futures Index.* 1984 was a year of confusion and ambivalence for the futures trader. The news and recommendations were almost universally bullish, and speculators bought into the first quarter rally on the assumption that prices were starting to head north. In reality, this brief advance was just a minor pause in the major bear trend that had gripped futures market since 1983 and would continue through 1985–86. Only the disciplined and pragmatic technical trades made money—and lots of it—on the short side of these markets.

entering a bearish scenario. Successful speculators, with a disciplined and pragmatic approach to trend analysis and utilizing a viable trend-following strategy, would have ignored all that market gossip and have focused instead, on a sound technical analysis. In so doing, they would have either scored some good profits on the short side or, at least, have avoided the long side and its attendant 'red ink.'

In summary, the frequent divergence between what one observes in an objective technical analysis, and what one reads in the so-called news and analysis, seems to provide a near-permanent feeling of ambivalence to many speculators. 'For example, it is generally difficult for the speculator to operate in the currency markets on the basis of funda-mental expectations or market gossip. Following weakness in currencies some time ago, the major New York financial papers noted, 'The US dollar surprised traders with a show of strength yesterday that stemmed, in part, from the detention of a Polish labor leader.' The

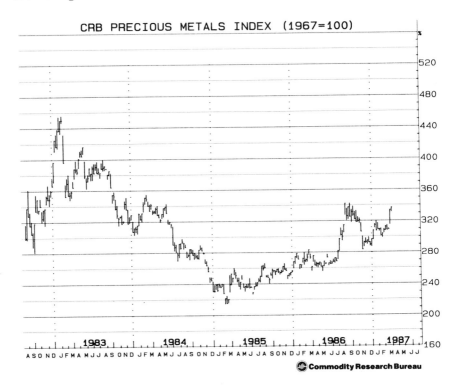

Figure 4.4 Precious Metals Index

Deutsch Mark was weak, which was attributed to the fact that German banks are major creditors of Poland. However, the Yen happened to be strong that day, so the same article deftly labelled its strength as a result of Japan's isolation from Europe. However, had the Yen declined, or had the Deutsch Mark advanced, you can be certain that an appropriately – worded rationale would have been created, and disseminated.

When I find myself becoming excessively confused or agitated by an excess of such obvious contradictions and contrived after-the-fact announcements and quasi-analysis, my response is to seclude myself from this so-called news. I focus, instead, on a detailed and pragmatic analysis of technical factors and indicators—trying to seek order amongst the chaos. Such an interval is always best conducted in seclusion, away from interruptions and well-intentioned advisors. There seems to be a correlation between the isolation and tranquility of the session and, the clarity and quality of the analysis.

5 The Art of War, by Sun Tzu (circa 506 BC) and The Art of Trading Success (circa AD 1994)

There are two books which I've read and re-read, at least five times each. The first is Livermore's *Reminiscences of a Stock Operator*, which describes his trading strategy and exploits. Obviously, Livermore is no longer a stranger to readers of this book. The other book is, *The Art of War*, by Sun Tzu, which is considerably more esoteric and obscure than Livermore. This is a work, written by a legendary Chinese general some 2,500 years ago. It was originally written as a treatise for victory on the field of battle, and if you read it literally, it is a story about men at arms, attacks by fire, ancient weapons and two-thousand-year-old battle tactics. But, this book, now read and studied worldwide, has greatly transcended its original purpose and intent.

The Art of War is arguably the most influential book of strategy in the world today, as enthusiastically studied in Asia by modern executives and politicians as it has been by military leaders and strategists for the last two millennia. In modern Japan, for example, leaders have applied the strategy outlined in this ancient classic to modern business and politics with astounding success. Indeed, some see in the successes of post-war Japan an illustration of Sun Tzu's dictum, 'to win without fighting is best.' Politics aside, *The Art of War* applies to competition in general, on every level from interpersonal to international. Its aim is invincibility, victory without battle, and unassailable strength through the understanding of physics, politics, the psychology of conflict and most importantly, the individual himself. *The Art of War* can be viewed against the background of the spiritual tradition of Taoism and can be the source of great insight into human nature and what makes some individuals succeed and others fail. Teaching that life is a complexity of interacting forces, Taoism has fostered both material and mental progress. Above all, *The Art of War* is a tool for understanding the very roots of conflict and resolution, of discipline and patience and, of success and failure. This is most eloquent and dramatic statement, to be sure. But, our interest is financial, not political or social. It is useful to review this book to see what it can offer by way of instruction to the stock and commodity speculator.

Sun Tzu wrote:

> 'If you know the enemy and know yourself, you need not fear the result of a hundred battles.'

Well, the longer you operate in financial markets, the more likely you are to see them as a vast battlefield and your campaigns, as battles. And although there are no great armies of archers or swordsmen waiting behind the next hill, you will, in the financial arena, find yourself in an alien, unfriendly universe with lots of participants ready to separate you from your capital and your self-condifence. You must know the markets thoroughly. Considerable experience is only half the battle; it must be accompanied by recall, to allow you to take advantage of the valuable lessons learned in past campaigns. In fact, the mere description of past markets as 'campaigns' lends additional credibility to the Sun Tzu type of references. As Sun Tzu said, you must know yourself, and nowhere is that more true than in financial speculation.

Sun Tzu said:

> 'The general who wins a battle makes many calculations in his temple before the battle is fought. The general who loses a battle makes but few calculations beforehand. Thus, many calculations lead to victory and few calculations lead to defeat.'

Have you noticed that, when you initiate or exit positions with little advance preparation, say on the basis of rumours, stories or tips, you are less likely to be successful than during those studied events where you calculate every known aspect of the event and base your ultimate decision on meticulous study of all such factors. Well, I certainly have observed this is my trading.

Sun Tzu said:

> 'When your weapons are dulled, your ardour dampened, your strength exhausted, and your treasure spent; then no man, however wise, will be able to avert the consequences that must ensue.'

Do not trade, or make investment decisions, unless you feel strong and confident that you can control the outcome of the event in bringing in big profits or small losses; and that, if you are not successful in this campaign, proceed to the next with the knowledge that, on balance, you have the confidence to know that you will be successful.

Sun Tzu said:

> 'The value of time — that is, being a little ahead of your
> opponent — has counted for more than either numerical
> superiority or the nicest calculations with regard to
> commissariat.'

When you are trading markets, whether you are a **day trader** or a
position trader, and you get an actionable signal from whatever
timing indicators you are using, make the trade, and make it fast!
While others are waiting to find out why a particular move is occurring,
you should be in there with your order entered, and ready to act on
whatever strategy you are using. This is a fast-paced game, and you
must be bold and ready to move, whenever your signals 'tell' you to go.
This is not the time to hesitate or be timid. Don't worry about being
wrong — your stops will protect you against big losses. But, nothing can
protect you against being timid after you get a valid trade signal from
a technical method that you believe in.

Sun Tzu said:

> 'When you capture spoils from the enemy, they must be used as
> rewards, so that all your men must have a keen desire to fight,
> each on his own account.'

Whenever I am in a difficult, extended campaign, and I do something
smart (or lucky), I usually reward myself with some tangible that
provides satisfaction. This might be a special dinner or, more recently,
I bought a camera that I had been admiring, from the winnings of a
very profitable trade. Perhaps the epitome of this strategy was when I
bought a beautiful custom 46-foot diesel powered sail-boat from the
winning of a huge **long** copper position that I had held, and suffered
with its ups and downs, for nine months. When the position was
ultimately closed, it gave me no end of satisfaction to write a cheque for
the full purchase price of the sail-boat.

Sun Tzu said:

> 'Plan for what is difficult while it is easy, do what is great while
> it is still small. The most difficult things in the world must be
> done while they are still easy, the greatest things in the world
> must be done while they are still small.'

It is a lot easier to plan a financial campaign in the quiet and security
of your office while you are still paper trading and preparing your
strategy. Every aspect of the total campaign should be studied and
calculated: what to do if prices advance or if they retreat; where and
how to add to the position (pyramid) and where and how to reduce the
size of the position; if the position turns sour do you just dump it, or

do you go into the market with the reverse position? These, and many other aspects of a trade should be analysed and worked out, in advance, before the intervention of big financial risks enter the picture. It is easy to do this in advance on paper; it becomes difficult once you have committed funds and put your money and your ego on the line.

Sun Tzu said:

'Strong action is training the body without being burdened by the body, exercising the mind without being used by the mind, working in the world without being affected by the world, carrying out tasks without being obstructed by tasks.'

We cannot trade to best advantage unless we are fit, both mentally and physically. Almost at one's best is not good enough. Success in trading, like success in sports competition, concert performance or playing in a chess match requires the utmost of physical and mental conditioning and concentration, focus and discipline. You'll know if you don't have it and in such cases, stand aside till you know that you're at your best. Likewise, do not permit external influences to intrude on your trading concentration. There was a magazine article about my trading style which pointed out that I once ignored a fire-drill in my office building; the truth was that I didn't even notice the fire alarm and people evacuating as I was so totally engrossed in the drama that was unfolding in the market-place and my anticipated response to various market occurrences.

Sun Tzu said:

'Greed is a fundamental cause of defeat; it is the unemotional, reserved, calm detached warrior who wins and not the ambitious seeker of fortune.'

In response to this, I turn to Jesse Livermore, who recounts how one of his high-flying trading buddies decided to buy his girlfriend a fur coat from his market profits. After several consecutive losses, someone else accepted the challenge and tried to 'win' the coat, but he too, was defeated. Eventually, others in the group tried it, all meeting the same fate, and eventually the project was dropped. The result was, the US\$2,000 coat had cost them collectively some US\$40,000 and, in the end, the coat went wanting. Winning at speculation is not an easy feat; but it is most practicable when you approach the speculative quest with reserve, detachment and total concentration. If you want to have fun and a good time, do something else for your excitement; when you operate in the market, be logical and serious.

And finally, Sun Tzu tells us the following regarding objectivity, assessing situations in a dispassionate manner and the advantages of carefully calculated action:

'Those who are skilled in combat do not become angered, those who are skilled at winning do not become afraid. Thus the wise win before they fight, while the ignorant fight to win.'

Let us return to Livermore, for a modern day analogy.

'Investors who can both be right and sit tight are uncommon. I found it one of the hardest things to learn. But it is only after a market operator has firmly grasped this that he can make big money. It is literally true that millions come easier to a trader after he learns to trade, than hundreds did in the days of his ignorance.'

6 That's the Way You Want to Bet

In a conversation with Larry Hite, a major world money manager, he noted that he didn't consider himself primarily in the commodity business. When I asked him what business he was in, he stated, 'the good bets.' Upon further reflection, he told me that a major part of his success was due to his ability to calculate the odds of winning in each position, and to place his bets (positions) accordingly.

This approach is pretty typical of professional traders, because I have never heard any non-professional trader expressing such theories. Yet, this is something that the non-professional should consider and learn more about, because it can be of definite help in operating successfully.

The title of this chapter is taken from the following quotation:

Damon Runyon
American writer

> 'The race doesn't always go to the swift,
>   Nor the battle to the strong,
> But that's the way you want to bet.'

What professional traders know, and what the above quotation suggests, is that the best 'play' is to bet on the favourite. The long shot, if it wins, pays off better than the favourite. But, the point is, the 'favourite' in most bets, is most likely to win. Surely, there are exceptions to this theory, and we can all recall instances where the long shot, paying off the big odds, has won a bet. But, such situations are definitely the exception. If you are looking for the best consistency in winning, you should consistently bet on the 'favourite.' Admittedly, on any one single 'bet,' the long shot may have a good chance of prevailing. But, winning just a single contest is not of particular interest to the serious speculator, who wants to be a consistent winner over a large number of 'bets.' And, this is where a consistent adherence to betting on the favourite, will pay off.

As an example, suppose you are betting on a tennis match, or a chess tournament. In both instances, the number one seed is playing against, say, the 20th seed. Surely, the favourite would have the smallest odds on him, while the long shot would carry much higher odds, and if he were to win, the pay-off would be impressive. Yet, the smart bet would be on the favourite. Any tournament-calibre player could beat the favourite in one, or just a few games, and this could be due to luck or some other circumstance. But, over a full-scale tennis or chess tournament, the long shot can't win on the basis of luck. This is where the favourite can be expected to win, and the experienced better would probably put his money on the favourite.

What about the time where you, or someone you know, took a long position in the market that was clearly in a major downtrend, or went short against a major uptrend; and the position resulted in a good profit? Is there a lesson to be learned in this? Does it mean if you consistently bought or sold against the major trends, you could expect to end up a winner? The answer is categorically, *no*!

I would like to suggest that profits in such anti-trend situations, if they occur, are primarily due to luck, and not to skill or trading acumen. Except for certain specific situations where very experienced traders utilize a strategy of anti-trend trading, one should restrict trading to the basic direction of the prevailing trend:

(a) Buy – minor-trend reactions in a major uptrend and
(b) Sell – minor-trend rallies in a major downtrend.

The following trade is typical of this trading with-the-trend strategy. Consider the case of the March NIKKEI, traded on the Singapore International Monetary Exchange (SIMEX) (see Figure 6.1).

In this analysis, we shall use the 50-day simple moving average (SMA) versus the closing price, as our trend indicator. We shall also take our **entry** and **exit** signals from the 9-day simple moving average versus the 18-day simple moving average versus the 50-day simple moving average:

Buy: close > 9-SMA > 18-SMA > 50-SMA.
Sell: close < 9-SMA < 18-SMA < 50 SMA.
Note: the symbol '>' means 'greater than.' The symbol '<' means 'less than.'

Examining this daily chart over the period March 1993 to February 1994, we can see that there were five distinct trend periods.

1. Uptrend; from March 1993 through mid-May 1993. Prices advanced from 17,200 to 21,000.

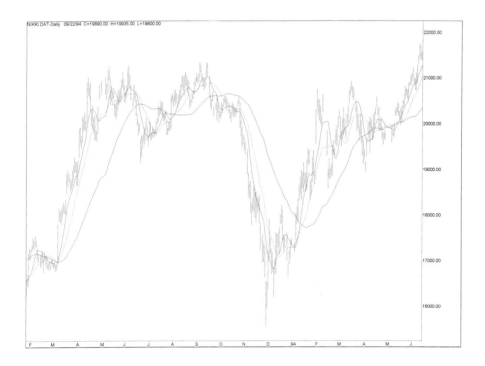

NIKKI.DAT-Daily 09/22/94 C=19890.00 H=19935.00 L=19800.00

Figure 6.1 Daily chart of NIKKEI (CASH) traded on SIMEX. This illustrates trends in action, because we have a top through late October, a steep downtrend through late November and then a gradual recovery to an uptrend through late March 1994.

2. Downtrend; June and July 1993. Prices declined from 21,000 to 19,200.

3. Uptrend; from June through early September 1993. Prices advanced from 19,400 to 21,000.

4. Downtrend; from early September 1993 to early January 1994, where prices declined from 21,000 to 16,000.

5. Uptrend; from January through June 1994, with prices advancing from 16,000 to 21,700.

Any speculator who traded this market in synch with the five phases as shown above, not only would have been on the right side of the markets (except for the two sideways trending periods when he probably would have been whipsawed, but with only moderate losses), but he would have scored good profits with relative consistency, and with just reasonable-size risks. Clearly, trend-following trading doesn't tend to buy at the lows or sell at the highs, and if that should happen it's due more to luck than to skill. Also, it tends to result in frustrating whipsaw losses during periods of sideways non-trending markets. But, it should get you aboard near enough to the highs and lows, in trending periods, to score some meaningful and consistent profits on both sides of the market.

Until someone discovers a better way for the non-professional speculator to trade, trend-following and betting on the favourite (a 'best bets' position) will probably continue to be the best approach to consistent and reasonable-risk trading. One other aspect to 'good bets' trading is utilizing a strategy for re-entering a trending market which you have exited prematurely.

Clearly, one of the imperatives in collecting big profits is the ability to sit on a with-the-trend position for the major part of a move, be it just a few months or even longer. This is easier said than done. There are many reasons why traders close out a position prematurely. These include getting stopped out on a too-close stop, or closing out due to boredom, impatience or nervousness. Also, the general psychology of dynamic markets is that the prevailing opinion is generally most bearish just before an upwards turn, and most bullish just before a downwards turn. 'No one ever goes broke taking a profit,' they say. My response is, 'no one ever gets rich taking a small profit in a big trending market.' We have all experienced this. We grab a small or intermediate profit and then, shortly thereafter, the market commences a major move, while we watch from the sidelines, with no position.

Livermore said it succinctly:

'Men who can both be right and sit tight are uncommon. I found it one of the hardest things to learn. But it is only after a market operator has firmly grasped this that he can make big money. It is literally true that millions come easier to a trader after he learns how to trade, than hundreds did in the days of his ignorance.'

The bottom line is, if you exit a trending position, regardless of the reason, and on the close of the next two days the trend is still in the original direction, you should get back aboard. And it doesn't matter materially if the price is higher or lower than where you exited.

There are different strategies for re-entering a market. You can place an order to re-enter the market US$200 on stop above the high of the day you exited (for a long position) or US$200 on stop below the low of the day you exited (for a short position). Alternatively you can use a short-term entry strategy, such as close versus 4-day versus 9-day simple moving averages, which can also be effective for getting you back aboard a good trending position. On getting back in the market, do not neglect to re-enter a protective stop, according to whatever stop strategy you have been using.

7 Those That Know Don't Tell; Those That Tell Don't Know

The title of this chapter is an old, respected truism in Wall Street. I first heard it from an experienced stock trader over 30 years ago when I was a neophyte Merrill Lynch account executive. It has been part of my professional strategy since I first learned it, for it is one of the few significant maxims in an industry where irrelevant slogans and sayings abound.

It's too bad that not enough financial operators practise this strategy. It could help traders and brokers in their speculative operations, especially in Asia, where so much of what passes for stock and commodity analysis depends largely on uninformed tips, rumours, stories and outright gossip. I would always put informed technical analysis over unconfirmed tips and stories.

I had an interesting experience recently, which exemplifies this point. The research director of a large Hong Kong investment firm showed me a price chart of some stock and asked for my opinion. 'If you are a buyer or a seller of this stock,' he asked me, 'how far would you project the stock to move?' My reply was simple and direct. 'I don't know.'

The gentleman was persistent and repeated the question. My reply was the same, but this time I answered in greater detail. 'I don't think that anyone could give you a competent answer, merely on the basis of a single price chart with no further information or technical studies.' Then I proceeded to suggest what additional information and studies I would want to examine before even attempting to analyse the chart.

'That's extremely interesting,' he replied. 'Do you know that I've shown the same chart to at least six other brokers and analysts, and every one of them gave me a definite answer with specific buy and sell points and even price objectives. And all of them combined would probably have less years of trading experience than you have.'

All I could say was, 'That's not surprising; it's what I would have expected.'

Jesse Livermore had a similar experience some 70 years ago. This is how he described it:

> 'I was at a dinner party one evening and was seated next to a man who had heard that I was in Wall Street. At one point in the conversation, he asked if I could tell him how one could make some quick money in stocks. Without answering the question, I asked what business he was in, and he said that he was a surgeon. I then asked if he could tell me how one could make some quick money in surgery.'

We are continuously forced to come to grips with the unique relationship between market news (stories, gossip and tips) versus actual market action. How many times has a company announce some very bullish piece of news – an increase in the dividend, improved earnings or some acquisition – and the public goes charging in to buy the stock? Then, after a few days of relative strength, the stock is in full retreat with all the recent buyers, having bought on the bullish news, sitting with big losses. How could that be? Wasn't the news very bullish? Perhaps the answer lies in the fact that the stock had already been going up for some time, with the 'insiders,' who knew about the impending announcement, having been big buyers of the stock before any bullish news was known. Then, the announcement was made and the public rushed in to buy. Who do you think supplied the stock for this (uninformed) buying? None other than the insiders, who were accumulating stock in advance of the news.

How can an investor, not privy to this information at the beginning of the move, protect himself? Well, had he taken the trouble to look before buying the stock, he would have observed that the market had been going up for some time in advance of the announcement. The big price surge on the basis of the anticipated bullish news (anticipated by the insiders, at least) provides these insiders with an opportunity to dump their large lines of long stock into a broadly surging market.

Stock buyers of IBM experienced this first hand, during the extended price decline from 1987 to 1993, when share prices declined from 175.00 to 40.00. At any number of times the stock was recommended by advisory services and brokerage firms, only to have it continue sliding relentlessly over a six-year period.

The sugar market, too, provides an excellent glimpse at the unique relationship between market news and market aciton. The way the news is released after every move should be studied by thoughtful investors. During an extended bear market in sugar, culminating around the 2.50 level in mid-1985, the decline was accompanied by

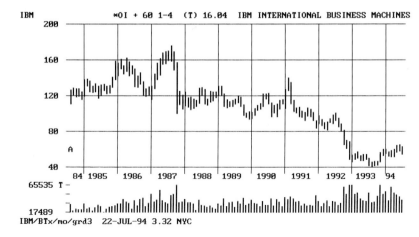

Figure 7.1 Long-term (monthly) stock chart of IBM, covering the period mid-1984 to mid-1994. Note the extended price decline from 175 to 40 over the six year period from 1987 to 1993.

every type of bearish news imaginable. But after the market had finally reversed and was moving **north**, the bearish news items were put back in the desk drawer and suddenly the bullish items were trotted out for dissemination. On 26 January 1987, following a protracted 200-point sugar rally (equal to a move of US$2,240 per contract on just a US$600 margin), *The Wall Street Journal* noted the following:

> 'Reports that the Soviet Union had been a large buyer of refined sugar in the world market helped futures to extend their advance . . . . Analysts said Moscow had bought 500,000 to 700,000 metric tons of raw sugar . . . and one analyst said the Soviets may buy as much as a million tons more. Analysts said prices were also buoyed by a report that Brazil will push back contracts to export 750,000 to 1,500,00 tons of raw sugar to 1988 or 1989 and by reports that Cuba is having problems harvesting and milling its cane sugar crop. In Brazil, diversion of sugar to alcohol production, stronger domestic consumption, and indications that drought may reduce the crop have created tight supplies, analysts said.'

The analysts seem to have 'trotted out' every bullish item they could think of after the market advanced. But you can be sure that, following the first big price decline, the 'news' would suddenly become totally bearish. One must wonder who these 'learned' analysts are who are always able to explain why a market made a move after the fact, but never seem to know, in advance, what to do.

And so it goes. The salient points to keep firmly in mind are firstly that market prices fluctuate and secondly that following every significant price move, analysts and commentators are to be heard offering perfectly plausible explanations for what just happened in the market. To many thoughtful observers, all this so-called news, floor gossip and rumour seems rather conveniently contrived by some of the professional and institutional operators in order to confuse and confound as many gullible traders as possible into taking untenable, anti-trend market positions.

There ought to be a way to avoid being caught in this recurring trap, and there is. The astute operator will ignore the plethora of rumours, **pit gossip** and what generally passes for market news. He will maintain his focus on the real technical factors underlying each market and on whatever disciplined strategy and risk control technique has worked best for him and for his particular style of investing or trading. He will not lose sight of the old Wall Street axiom:

'Those That Know Don't Tell; Those That Tell Don't Know.'

8 Why There is No Such Thing as a 'Bad' Market

A letter that I received from a professional trader bears special significance, as it relates to the subject of this chapter.

> 'We have been hearing quite a bit about the difficulty of trading current markets. No sooner does the trend "flip" on many of the technical and computer systems that traders use, and of course, the majority of speculators quickly take positions on the "new trend," than the market suddenly reverses again and goes racing the opposite way. It seems to be a recurring stream of bad markets, and it is happening with increasing regularity. What can the trader do about this?'

This happens to many traders, who become extremely perplexed, and who want to know how to handle these 'bad' markets.

It is unfortunate, but true, that when an investor makes money he attributes it to skill, superior acumen and clever timing. But when he loses money, he tends to rationalize it thus; the market was terrible, too volatile and excessively choppy. Speculators tend to overlook, or to deny, the real causes of losing trades.

It is difficult to admit to misjudgement of the market trend, the trade timing, the placement of stops or the tactical market approach. Only by acknowledging such errors frankly can we discover where and how we erred and how to avoid such mistakes next time.

The universal truth about futures markets is that, except for occasional and unusual brief time periods, the market and the price trends are not, in themselves, good or bad, right or wrong. It is the trader himself who is good or bad, or more specifically, right or wrong. This general commentary probably goes back to the beginning of commodity trading, as many as 50 centuries ago. Even in those ancient days, the winners probably called the markets 'good,' while the losers

41

called them 'bad.' In fact, during choppy and apparently randomly moving trends, with unexpected reversals, and then reversals-from-reversals, it is more important than ever to play a disciplined and objective game. We all get whipsawed from time to time, but it is important not to let such markets upset or unnerve you.

During much of 1993, I got whipped in a good-sized Nikkei futures position, despite my best resolutions to play 'by the rules.' I had been **short a line** of March Nikkei futures, during the period April to September 1993, anticipating a break in the market. I should have noticed that the market was locked within a broad sideways trading range bounded by 20,000 and 21,500. After a few vain attempts to catch the trend I realized that there wasn't one, or to put it more accurately, that the trend was sideways and that I should have waited on the sidelines. In any event, by mid-October, I was tired of watching the 'red ink' all over my statements, and I opted to sit the Nikkei out from the safety of the sidelines. That was just before the market finally collapsed the last week of October 1993, and in very short order, declined from 20,000 top 16,000 – with me watching increduluously from the sidelines.

Yet, during such frustrating and difficult periods, there are always lots of clear thinking and disciplined operators whose accounts appreciate nicely, no small feat during periods of mostly sideways market and listless trends. One of the emotional problems that traders have to face, in terms of being right or wrong, is the subconscious reversal of two basic human emotions; hope and fear.

1. Trader A is **long** soybeans in the direction of the major (up) trend and is sitting with a good profit. He sells on the first reaction, **fearing** that if he continues to hold his long position the market may reverse to down and he will lose his profit.

2. Trader B, on the other hand, is **short** soybeans against the major (up) trend, and is sitting with a small but growing loss. He will probably sit with the losing position, **hoping** that the market will reverse its major uptrend (it probably won't reverse, at least while he, and others like him, remain short, and start moving **south**). In the meantime, the market continues its major uptrend and his loss continues to mount.

What we are experiencing are our principal emotions of hope and fear, but disoriented by 180 degrees. Trader A, with his profitable long position, should sit tight, hoping that the favourable moving market will continue advancing in his direction, adding to his profits. Trader B, on the other hand, sitting with an unprofitable anti-trend position,

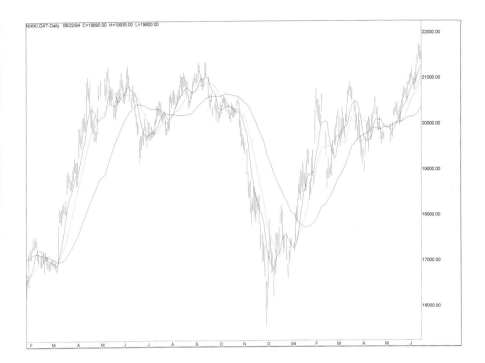

Figure 8.1 Daily chart of NIKKEI (CASH) traded on SIMEX. This illustrates trends in action, because we have a top through late October, a steep downtrend through late November and then a gradual recovery to an uptrend through late March 1994.

should close out, fearing that the adverse trend will continue (as it usually does) and the loss will continue to increase (it too, usually does).

The trend of a market is a lot like the weather; it is what it is, and there's not much anyone can do to change it. Or, as Mark Twain once said: 'Everybody talks about the weather, but no one does anything about it.' So, if the weather looks like rain, you wear a raincoat or carry an umbrella, whether you like it or not. Similarly, if the trend of a market is down, you play it short, or aside; and if the trend is up, you play it long, or aside — because you can't change the basic trend direction of the market. You either go with the trend, or you suffer the probable losses in trying to buck the trend.

There will be those instances when the market trend is down, your position is long, and somehow you end up making money. Or, the trend of the market is up, you go long, and you end up losing money. Do those experiences contradict the oft-stated strategy, 'go with the trend?' Not at all. There are exceptions to every rule, and those types of trades, where you go against the trend and make profits, or you go with the trend and lose money, are merely exceptions to the rule. In like manner, you may see a golfer reverse his normal grip on the club and sink the putt. Does that mean that this is the way to play golf? Not at all. It is just that it worked once, but if he were to try such a stunt over a period of time, the results would undoubtedly be otherwise.

It is only human to become discouraged when trading goes badly. Despite the best intentions and attempts at an objective and disciplined approach, most trades turn out losers. We all have moments like these, myself included. I have found that the best strategy for such periods is to close out all positions and stand aside from the market, for as long as it takes to get your head cleared and your attitude to become more positive. The market will be there, you can be sure, when you return to action. I am reminded of a story told about Dickson Watts, a famous old-time cotton trader from the 19th century. When asked for advice by a fellow-trader who claimed that the large size of his position kept him awake at night, Watts had the following to-the-point advice: 'sell down to a sleeping level.' It is still a sound advice.

9 Perception versus Reality

In any serious financial speculation one must be aware of reality and perception; and more importantly, be able to objectively distinguish between the two. For example, every time you take a with-the-trend position, you should premise that you are in for a mega-move. By so doing, you will be encouraged to hold the position and not look for short-term trades. Here is perception versus reality. Your perception tells you to hold every with-the-trend position, looking for the big move. Your sense of reality tells you that most trades are not destined for the big move. But, since you don't know in advance which trade will be wildly successful and since you know that some of them will be, the strategy of choice is to assume each with-the-trend trade can be the 'big one'; and let your stops take you out of those trades which fizzle.

This strategy can be illustrated with an example. Situation 'A' occurs in the World Trade Center building, in New York. Imagine you are in a lift with two other men, one of whom you recognize as a leading money manager of equities. You and he have never met, but his reputation as a dynamic and usually-right money manager is legendary.

The LMM (Legendary Money Manager) is talking to his companion: 'Charlie, I want you to buy 100,000 shares of XYZ this afternoon; it's trading around US$40.00.'

Charlie, whom you surmise to be one of his dealers replies: 'Sure thing, boss. But what's up? What are you looking for in the stock?'

The LMM replies: 'Looks like there's a little technical squeeze about to happen. I'm not looking for much of a move, so if you see, say, ten points in it, grab the profit.'

End of conversation, as the two men get off at the 43rd floor, and you continue up to your office on the 46th.

When you reach your office, you sit down for a minute to consider the situation. You think about the 'tip' you just heard, and make an assessment of whether the conversation was genuine or whether they staged it just to draw you into the market. You conclude that it was a genuine conversation. So, you call your stockbroker. 'Pete, what's going on in XYZ?' you inquire.

'Strange you should ask,' replies the broker, 'there's some good buying coming in, and the stock just jumped from 39½ to 41 on big volume; no one seems to know why.'

'Very interesting,' you respond. 'Pete, please buy 500 shares for me, at the market. Call me back with the fill.'

In a few minutes, you get a return call from the broker confirming that you've just bought 500 shares of XYZ, 300 at 41¼ and the remaining 200 at 41½. The stock is now 41½ bid offered at 42.

You then start to follow the stock, which closes that day at 44, again on heavy volume; and, opens the following morning at 45¼ on a large block. The stock continues strong for a few days but, on Friday, it seems to be running out of steam, opening at 52 for a new high, but closing down at 49, the first day in the week that it opened on a high and then closed down at the low.

On Monday, it opened on a downside gap, at 48¼.

It is important to digress and discuss the strategy here. What would you do, if you were the investor in the story, sitting with the 500 shares? Recapping the situation: you bought XYZ because of an overheard conversation between a legendary money manager, who said he was looking for just ten points, and his dealer. You could easily expect that the dealer may be bailing out with his anticipated ten-point profit and that if you held the position, you could find the stock back at the original US$42 price wondering why you never sold the stock to grab the easy profit. So, what would you do?

Well, I don't know what 'you' would do, but if it were me, I'd dump the 500 shares at the market. The stock did what you expected of it, so get off the 'train' and look for another ride.

End of Situation 'A.'

However, that wasn't what really happened – it was just a story. The actual story follows and it's considerably more interesting.

This story begins exactly the same way. The money manager and his dealer are in the same lift with you and you do overhear a conversation, although not the exact same conversation:

The LMM is talking to his dealer: 'Charlie, I want you to buy 100,000 shares of XYZ this afternoon; it's trading around US$40.00.'

Charlie replies: 'Sure thing, boss. But, what's up. What are you looking for in the stock?'

As you can see, until now, both conversations have been identical, but here they diverge.

Back to the LMM: 'I think there's a big move in the offing. I'm looking for the stock to double by the end of the year. And, if you get the first 100,000 shares around US$40.00, pick up an additional 50,000 shares if it gets to US$55.00.'

End of conversation, as the two men get of at the 43rd floor and you continue up to your office on the 46th.

Let's review now: this part of the story is the same. You assess whether the conversation you just overheard was genuine and, assuming that it was, you call your stockbroker and ask him to buy 500 shares. From here, the story continues just as before, except for the part about what you would do with the stock. Well, what would you do? It is a pity this isn't some form of interactive TV. But since it isn't, I can't hear your response. So, permit me to tell you what I would do.

I would hold the stock, and not even consider selling shares on the minor reaction back to 48½. Matter of fact, I would consider buying more shares on, say, a 50% to 60% reaction from the recent trading high.

Well, there you have it. The actual market action is identical in both instances. Yet, in situation 'A,' you (I) would look to dump the 500 shares on the reaction to 48½. But, in situation 'B,' you (I) hold the stock, and would in fact, probably buy more shares on any further extension of the price reaction. You must be ready to ask, why am I telling these stories and, what are the significant differences between actions we would take in situations 'A' and 'B?' What has all this to do with investment strategy and, ultimately, is there a lesson to be learned here?

Let's start by answering the last question: it has everything to do with investment strategy and, if you learn this lesson well, and practise it consistently, your speculative results should be greatly improved. The significant difference between the two scenarios has more to do with perception than reality. The actual facts of the two scenarios are essentially similar. You overheard a conversation in which a money manager told his dealer to buy 100,000 shares of a particular stock. The difference between the two situations is that, in the first instance, you were anticipating a small, short-term advance and you quickly dumped the stock based on that perception. In the second situation, your expectation, based solely on an overheard conversation, was that the stock could experience a very substantial up-move, possibly doubling in price. Accordingly, your tactical conclusion was to hold the position despite the price reaction, and to even buy more on further reaction. This conclusion was based entirely on your perception of an anticipated major price move.

Your initial action to buy 500 shares were identical. But your subsequent actions were entirely different, based solely on your expectation or perception that the stock could have a major move, rather than merely a short-term rally.

In reality the significance of this is that every time you assume a market position in the direction of the major trend (and having a with-the-trend-position is the critical factor), you should premise that the market could have major profit potential and you should play your strategy accordingly, as you did in situation 'B.' Now, before you rush forward to inform me that most market situations, in reality, are not destined for the big move, I will certainly concede that point. But, who can predict, in advance, which situation does, and which does not, have major profit potential (remember, we are restricting this discussion solely to markets in line with the major market trend)?

The annals of financial markets are replete with real time examples of markets that started most unimpressively, but then developed into full scale mega-moves. Meanwhile, most of the original participants, who may have climbed on board at the very inception of the move, got out at the first profit opportunity and then watched as the market continued to move very substantially, but certainly without them.

A good case in point was the cotton market in 1993 and 1994. Cotton futures commenced an advance from around the 60.00 level in October 1993 and I had a good-sized long position. There was substantial long-term resistance around 70.00, and I took profits on half of my position, thinking I would hold the other half for the long pull. Well, despite the best of intentions, something in the market distracted me and I sold out the balance of the long position, still around 70.00. As you can see from the chart (Figure 9.1), the market wasn't much impressed by my liquidation, because prices roared past me, right up to the 77.00 level and I watched on without any position in the market.

Some of my biggest profits in futures have been in copper and wheat, where I held long positions for eight to ten months. My winnings on these with-the-trend positions were substantially more than US$1 million each. But, my longest holding period, and I would like to hear from any reader who has been able to continuously hold a position for longer, was in world sugar, back in the 1970s. I got long of sugar, around the 2.00 level back in 1969 and held it (kept rolling the positions forward, and at times got stopped out, but re-entered) for some five years till 1974, ultimately liquidating near the 60.00 level.

Jesse Livermore tells a story about a famous old speculator, Partridge, who was a long-term stock holder. At times, other traders would give him tips, and then ask him what he thought they should do. He always listened intently, and finally he would say, 'you know, it's a bull market,' or, 'you know, it's a bear market,' as though he was giving them a precious piece of wisdom. Once a fellow trader went up

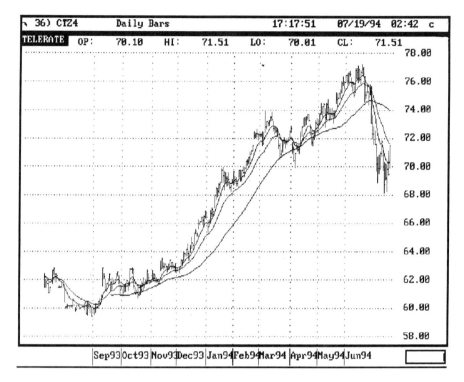

```
36) CTZ4          Daily Bars                17:17:51   07/19/94  02:42  c
TELERATE    OP:   70.10   HI:   71.51   LO:   70.01   CL:   71.51
                                                                        78.00
                                                                        76.00
                                                                        74.00
                                                                        72.00
                                                                        70.00
                                                                        68.00
                                                                        66.00
                                                                        64.00
                                                                        62.00
                                                                        60.00
                                                                        58.00
         Sep93 Oct93 Nov93 Dec93 Jan94 Feb94 Mar94 Apr94 May94 Jun94
```

Figure 9.1 Daily chart of DECEMBER 1994 COTTON. Major price moves tend to go further and longer than most traders anticipate. Don't be in a rush to close out or reverse a position until you have distinct technical signals to support the move.

to Partridge and told him that he was selling his position in Climax Motors, because he heard it was heading lower, and he could then buy back his stock at a lower price. He advised Partridge to do the same. 'My dear boy,' said old Partridge, in great distress, 'if I sold that stock now I'd lose my position, and then where would I be?'

Partridge was holding 500 shares with a 7 point profit, for a total profit of US$3,500. The tipster was nonplussed. 'Can you beat that?' he said. 'He bought 500 shares and now he has a US$47.00 profit; I tell him to sell out and rebuy after the decline, and he tells me he can't do it because he would lose his job.'

'I beg your pardon, Mr Harwood,' responded Partridge. 'I didn't say I would lose my job. I said that I would lose my position . . . my stock position in Climax Motors; and I don't want to do that.'

Livermore than went on to say, that what Partridge meant was that in a bull market, he didn't want to take the risk of not being able to buy back his stock. Livermore then pointed out, that a long-term holder speculating with the trend, should not try to capture small counter-trend profits by trying to get in and get out, because ultimately, the market would run away with the trader just sitting there on the sidelines. Livermore's final admonition should be a good warning to all traders:

> 'I know that if I tried to trade against my position by taking the counter-trend moves, I might lose my position, and with it the certainty of making a big killing with the big move. It is the big swing that makes the big money for you.'

10 Risk Control and Discipline: Keys to Success

In the jungle, for all creatures large and small, the first priority is survival. This should apply to financial speculators, as well. Here however, 'survival' is translated as 'risk control' and 'discipline.' The quest for profits is important, but even this basic drive takes second place to the dual imperatives of risk control and discipline. The Scots have an old saying, 'Mind your pennies and the pounds will take care of themselves.' The corollary to this in financial speculation is, 'Mind your losses and the profits will take care of themselves.'

There are a number of excellent books which describe the strategies and techniques of the leading portfolio investors of our time. These are fascinating accounts of a diverse group of talented men and women, whose investment feats have made them highly acclaimed experts throughout the various sectors of investments. Studying these accounts, one is struck by the wide ranging expertise of these 'money masters' and 'market wizards': stock speculation, long-term value investing, **short-term scalping**, **options strategies** and currency or bond trading. In fact, just about every one of these experts plies his or her personal operations quite differently from the others. There is hardly a single common element in their professional activities; with one exception. Each one of them acknowledges that **risk control** and **discipline** are clearly the two most significant aspects of their overall success. The single element on which they all agree.

Clearly, for every investor who reads this book, regardless of the field of investment he or she focuses on, the most important tactic for consistent and successful speculation is to control losses, also known as risk control, and discipline to 'trade by the rules.' If you can control losses and allow profits to run, and that is not easy to accomplish, you can be a consistent winner. What should be sought is a systematic, objective approach to risk control and discipline, which would include the following three areas:

1. Limit Your Risk on Each Position
   (a) One approach is to establish a maximum loss limit on each market, to say, 1% to 3% of your capital, the precise amount depending on the size of the account. For smaller accounts, it might not be practical to try to limit losses to 1%, as your stops would be so tight as to result in a string of losses due to whipsaw moves. There's nothing magic about this specific technique; it just helps enforce a discipline to control losses in an objective and systematic manner.
   (b) Another approach is to equate risk on each position to the respective exchange minimum margin and to limit risk to a percentage of such margin. Equating acceptable risk to a percentage of margin is a logical strategy, especially in futures trading, where margins are set by each exchange and are generally related to the volatility, and indirectly, to the risk or profit potential of each market. For example, on the Chicago Board of Trade, the world's principal grain futures exchange, the margin on a 5,000 bushel contract of corn is US$400, while the margin on a 5,000 bushel contract of soybeans, considered a more volatile and high-flying market, is US$800. If, for example, your risk is limited to 70% of margin, you would risk US$560 on soybeans versus US$280 on corn because your profit potential would be higher on soybeans than on corn.
   (c) Stock traders can limit speculative trading risks based on the value of the investment, but the precise amount would depend on the volatility of the stock, with a more volatile stock requiring somewhat looser stops. Such loss limits could be between 15% to 20% of the investment. Thus a trade in a US$30.00 stock could be stopped to limit losses to US$4.50 to US$6.00.
   (d) Also, one should not use more than one-third of the capital in a speculative trading account to margin positions, keeping two-thirds in reserve, to be held at interest, as a cushion. If the account equity declines, you should seek to reduce positions, so as to retain this recommended one-third ratio.

2. Avoid Overtrading
This admonition pertains to both excessive trading activity, such as churning, and to putting on too large a position in relation to the capital in an account. You aren't likely to trade successfully if you are

overtrading, or if you are excessively focused on short-term scalping, or if the first adverse swing will have you responding to a margin call.

3. Cut Your Losses

Any time you enter a speculative, trading position, you should clearly know where your **bail out point** (stop loss) will be and you should enter the stop with your broker. Experienced traders who sit in front of an online monitor and who have the discipline to dump a position when and if it reaches their bail out point, may not actually want to put the stop to the floor, especially if they are holding a substantial position, as it could be a magnet to attract floor traders' attention to hitting the stop. The key aspect here is discipline, because not entering the stop should never be used as an excuse for overstaying a market, or for rationalizing any delay in liquidating at the designated stop point.

Assuming a newly entered position starts to move against you from the outset, the stop, if entered correctly, should get you out with just a reasonable loss. However, what should you do about stop protection if the market starts to move favourably, putting paper profits in your account? Clearly, you will want to adopt some strategy to advance the stop so that a good paper profit doesn't turn into a big loss if the market reverses. Here, the maxim to focus on is, 'never allow a good profit to turn into a loss.' But, how exactly should this be handled? One recommended strategy is to advance your stop (if long, raise the stop; if short, lower the stop) after each Friday's close, by an amount equal to 50% of the week's favourable move. For example, if you are short gold and the market declines by US$10.00 during one week, you would lower your buy stop by US$5.00 as of Friday's close. However, if a market moves against you on any week, you should leave the previous week's stop intact. Eventually, the market will reverse and stop you out; but if you have enjoyed a good run, you will have advanced into a no-loss stop position and, ultimately, a profitable one.

11 Long-term versus Short-term Trading

I am frequently asked which is more profitable, long-term or short-term trading. Obviously, there are pros and cons to each approach, and my answer is, you should use whichever works best for you. In my own trading, however, I adhere to a dual strategy. That is, I am a long-term trader on my winning positions and a short-term trader on my adverse ones. That makes sense to me. If the market is moving favourably (your position is with the prevailing trend) and your trading is profitable, hold the position for as long as possible. Don't try to **pick off tops and bottoms**, because it isn't possible to do it with any degree of consistency. But, if you determine that your position is counter to the prevailing trend and the loss is becoming bigger, get out as soon as possible.

How long should you hold a profitable position? As long as possible. My biggest profits, in both wheat and copper, have been on positions held about nine months and I once held a long position in sugar for five years. Of course I had to roll the long position over as each future expired and occasionally was stopped out by an extreme counter-trend reaction, but I got back aboard each time as quickly as possible.

If it seems more difficult to make good long-term profits than it used to be, the fault is less with the markets and more with the players. The focus of most technical traders, in both securities and commodities, has become increasingly short-term and micro-oriented, due mainly to two factors:

- Increased volatility and seemingly random price action resulting from enormous sums of speculative money being thrown at markets that lack sufficient breadth and institutional participation to cope with the huge influx of orders.

55

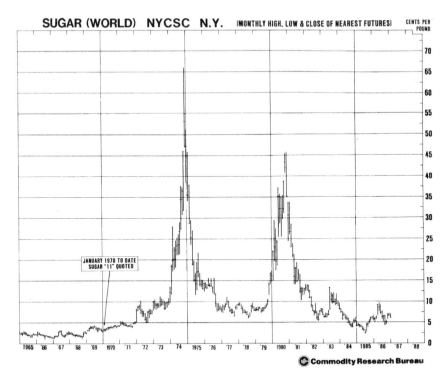

Figure 11.1 Long-Term Monthly (Nearest Future) Sugar. Talk about
needing patience! I accumulated a big long position in 1967–68 around
the 2.00 level, right before it plummeted to 1.33. I lost some one third of
the position on this drop, and held on to long sugar for two years before
the market broke out of its long sideways range and started moving up.
Once on the move, however, the bull market lasted five years, culminating
at the 60.00-plus level in late 1974.

- The proliferation of powerful micro-computers and software
  programmes that focus on short-term trading swings, convincing
  many technical operators that this is the new wave of the
  marketplace and the preferred way to trade.

Indeed, this is the day of the tick-by-tick computerized chart,
continuously on-line and updating during every moment of each
trading session. For only a modest monthly expense, virtually any
trader can now have five minutes (or less) bar charts, with any number
of technical indicators interposed on the charts, flashing across his
colour monitor in rapid succession, or being printed on hard copy. Just
imagine, trading against a 'triple top' formation created during a single
30 minute segment of a trading session.

I had a graphic demonstration of this micro-analysis recently, when
a trader called to ask what I thought about the 'head and shoulders' top

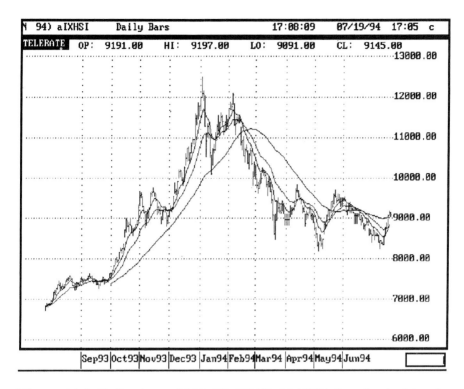

Figure 11.2 Daily chart of HANG SENG (CASH.) Imagine looking for a head and shoulders top formation in early December 1993 at the 9,937 level.

formation he had identified in Hang Seng. I could only reply with 'what head and shoulders top are you talking about? Which market are you talking about?' In fact, I had been watching the same market he had been referring to, solidly entrenched in a strong and dynamic uptrend. I was long this market and I hadn't detected anything remotely resembling a top formation. Under further questioning from me, the gentlemen admitted that his 'top formation' had occurred during a brief period that morning. I reminded him that he was watching a very minute price consolidation taking place within an ongoing strong bull trend and that I wasn't very impressed with his analysis. I advised him to look for a spot to buy, rather than to sell. The market apparently, shared my opinion, for by the close, we were registering new highs. The triple top formation had been sundered as if it didn't exist, which it didn't! (See Figure 11.2.)

This trader's micro-oriented approach to short-term scalping is the exact opposite of long-term position trading, which provides the best opportunities for consistent profits and limited risk. Adhering to a

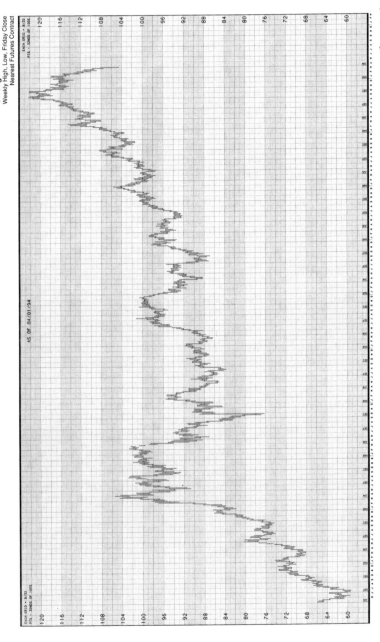

Figure 11.3 Long term (monthly) chart of U.S. BONDS. A careful review of long term charts can often help the trader get a better overall balanced perspective of a market. Reprinted with permission © 1994 Knight-Ridder Financial; 30 South Wacker Drive Suite 1820, Chicago, Illinois 60606.

strategy of focusing primarily on the longer-term trends allows one to avoid being distracted by intra-day market 'noise' and to maintain a better perspective on market trend action. How can the trader sitting in front of a five-or-three-minute tick-by-tick chart have any balanced perspective of a market? Three or four hours is long-term to him.

For most of the market which I follow, I find particular usefulness in reviewing long-term charts, that is, weekly and even monthly bar charts. Such a longer-term view tends to provide me with a better balanced perspective of market action. I sometimes wonder how many people watch such long-term charts and indicators, versus those who follow short-term five and ten minutes, or even tick-by-tick charts. Not very many, I should think.

Merging short-term and long-term techniques into a trading strategy

For aggressive and experienced traders, there is an interesting approach which involves combining short- and long-term indicators into a viable trading method. The first step is to identify the major, prevailing trend of each market. There are as many different techniques of trend identification as there are traders and indeed, many operators simply use a subjective inspection of a chart as the basis for determining trend direction. This may be useful and accurate, in the hands of an experienced and disciplined operator but for many observers, it is entirely too subjective and discretionary an approach. Most traders have some degree of market bias. For instance, I admit to being biased towards the long side of soybean futures and if given a neutral type of trend analysis, I am much more prone to buy than to sell. What we seek here is a neutral, unbiased and objective approach to trend analysis.

At the outset it should be noted that the particular moving average values presented here are not the ones I specifically use. They are presented for illustration only, as they are close to, and representative of, the moving average values that are used by many successful traders. Each trader will have to test technical methods to derive the indicators and formulae which best suit his purposes and his trading style.

One particular method, simple and straightforward, that some traders use for long-term trend indentification is a 50-day simple moving average versus the close of a daily bar chart. It works as follows:

1. The trend is up if:
   (a) The closing price is above the moving average line and
   (b) The slope of the moving average line is up.

2. The trend is down if:
   (a) The closing price is below the moving average line and
   (b) The slope of the moving average line is down.

There are a multitude of trend identification methods, some of which are very complicated, but this is quite simple and it is more effective than most methods. Another advantage of this method is that it is objective and totally unbiased. As a purely mathematical approach, it is simple and direct. Furthermore, sideways markets tend to show a non-directional moving average line that is close to being equivalent to the price line. These markets are deemed sideways, and should be avoided for this particular trend-following strategy.

From this objective method of trend identification it is possible to formulate the following rules:

- In an uptrend, carry long positions only, or else stand aside. No short positions.
- In a downtrend, carry short positions only, or else stand aside. No long positions.

The next step is to formulate entry and exit rules and for this discussion, we will use the following rules:

- For long-term analysis use the close versus three simple moving averages: 10-day, 20-day and 50-day.
  — Buy when close > 10-day > 20-day > 50 day.
  — Sell when close < 10-day < 20-day < 50 day.
- For short-term analysis, use the close versus three simple moving averages, 4-day, 9-day and 18-day.
  — Buy when close > 4-day > 9-day > 18-day.
  — Sell when close > 4-day > 9-day > 18-day.

To coordinate the total strategy:

- In an uptrend (using the 50-day simple moving average) buy on the long-term signal, that is; close > 10-day > 20-day > 50-day.
  Stop out the trade (liquidate only, do not go short) using the short-term signal, that is; close < 4-day < 9 day < 18-day.
  If you are stopped out and the trend continues up (based on the 50-day simple moving average) re-enter long on the short-term buy signal, that is; close > 4-day > 9-day > 18-day.
- In a downtrend (using the 50-day simple moving average) sell on the long-term signal, that is; close < 10-day < 20-day < 50-day.
  Stop out the short position (liquidate only, do not go long) using

the short-term signals, that is; close < 4-day < 9-day < 18-day. If you are stopped out and the trend continues down (based on the 50-day simple moving average) re-enter short on the short-term sell signal, that is; close < 4-day < 9-day < 18-day.

For additional stop protection, you might use an exit stop based on 70% of margin, in case the indicator-based reversal flip is slow in getting you out.

To summarize long-term trend analysis:

- The basic long-term trend is determined by the 50-day simple moving average versus the closing price.
- If the trend is up, trade long or stand aside. No short positions.
- If the trend is down, trade short or stand aside. No long positions.
- If your basic long position is stopped out, using the short-term strategy, do not go short. If the 50-day simple moving average remains long, re-buy the position on a buy signal from the short-term strategy.
- If your basic short position is stopped out, using the short-term strategy, do not go long. If the 50-day simple moving average remains short, re-sell the position on a sell signal from the short-term strategy.

12 Buy the Strength; Sell the Weakness

The first half of this decade has witnessed some of the toughest and most frustrating financial markets in recent memory. Good trading strategy holds that you should be able to profit equally in both up and down markets. But, during many campaigns, markets have appeared to be moving both up and down nearly simultaneously. Many solid uptrends have been punctuated with violent downside reactions. These price slides briefly halt the uptrend by stopping out speculative long positions and after the stops have been 'cleaned out,' the market resumes its northerly course. Conversely, quite a few bear trends have experienced equally violent rallies. The rally cleans out the speculative protective buy stops, knocking the so-called weak holders out of their profitable short positions; then the bear market resumes.

The attention of the margin department is being noticed more frequently than ever before due to the erratic and violent nature of counter-trend swings. What should you do when confronted with the ever-familiar call for additional margin? Over the many years, I have had countless conversations with traders, both in stocks and futures, concerning the strategy of dealing with margin calls. In general, most investors are ambivalent and inconsistent in their response to margin calls and require guidance in terms of a viable, strategic response. There are two types of calls: **new business** and **maintenance**. Exchange regulations generally require that new business calls be met with the deposit of new funds, not by liquidation. Maintenance calls, however, can be met with either deposit of new funds or by reducing positions.

Maintenance calls are the most common type of margin call and it is unfortunate that most investors invariably make the wrong decision when confronted with the request for additional margin. There are two options: putting up new money, or reducing positions. If reducing positions, a decision on which one(s) should be liquidated to meet the call should be made. In most circumstances I do not recommend depositing new funds to meet a maintenance call. The call is a clear sign that the account is underperforming, or at least some of the positions are underperforming, and there is no logic in trying to defend bad positions with fresh money. The appropriate strategy is to liquidate some positions to eliminate the margin call and to reduce your risk exposure. But, if you close positions to reduce risk, aren't you also reducing your profit potential and your ability to regain a profitable footing? Reducing positions, yet maintaining and even enhancing your profit potential sounds like a worthwhile although hypothetical goal; but how can you actually achieve it? It can be done with a simple and basic strategy that is well known to successful professional traders but unfortunately, not to public speculators. Those positions which show the biggest paper losses when **marked to the market**, should be closed out especially if they are moving anti-trend. This clearly reduces risk exposure. Yet, by maintaining the most profitable positions, which are trending in the direction of the dominant market trend and possibly even adding to those positions (pyramiding), you are maintaining your potential for profit. The odds clearly favour ultimate investment success on profitable with-the-trend positions over losing anti-trend positions.

Regrettably, most speculators choose to close out their profitable positions while holding on to the losing ones. How many times have we heard the statement, 'I can't afford to take the loss.' The likely outcome of this attitude is that, when the position is ultimately liquidated, the loss is greater than it would have been earlier in the game. The strategy of closing profitable positions while holding on to losing ones is costly and is typical of unsuccessful traders. Conversely, one of the traits of successful operators is to close out losing positions and stay with, and even add to, the winning ones. And, while it may be more gratifying to take profits rather than losses, we should not be concerned with satisfying the ego here. We should be playing for big profits coupled with limited risks and, in that context, you should be more concerned with an overall profitable operation than in trying to prove yourself right and the market wrong.

There is another corollary here that professional operators use. In any given market, or in two related markets, you should buy the strongest acting one and sell the weakest acting one. This tends to hedge your bet in a constructive fashion, because if the market advances, your long leg should outperform your short leg; while, if the market declines, your short leg, being the weaker-acting of the two, should go down faster and further. And, in some markets, futures for example, you may get an accompanying bonus, with reduced **straddle** (spread) margins.

The strategy of buying the strength; selling the weakness can be exemplified by the Chicago corn market which was in a broad downtrend from late 1983 to early 1987. The wheat market, on the other hand, was trending generally higher, providing technical, or systems traders, with a succession of highly reliable and straightforward trading signals. Let us assume you received a sell signal in corn during June 1986 and put on a short position. Your margin in each 5,000 bushels corn contract would have been US$400. Then you received a buy signal in wheat in October of the same year and bought a contract. The margin on each wheat contract would have been US$600, so for your combined short corn and long wheat position you would expect to have to **post** US$1,000 in margin. You may be surprised to learn that you wouldn't have to post this amount or even US$600, the higher of the two legs. It is possible to put on the entire two-sided position (short

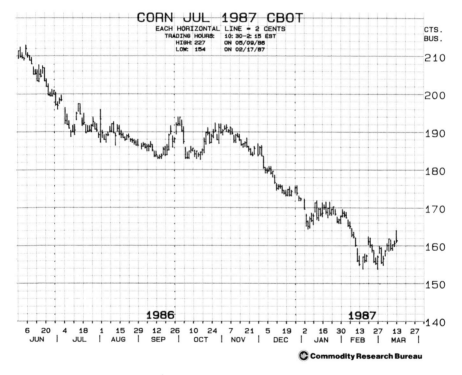

Figure 12.1 July 1987 Corn. You buy the strength (wheat) and sell the weakness (corn). This is the type of situation that many professional operators seek; it has good profit potential, reasonable risk, and low margin. Opportunities like this appear every year—and the trader should be alert to the chance to buy the strength and sell the weakness. For entry timing, you can take signals from whichever technical or trading system you have confidence in and time each leg on the basis of these signals.

corn and long wheat) for a total margin of just US$500. Generally however, it is not advisable to trade on such a thin margin and in this example, at least the US$600 required on the higher side (wheat) should be deposited, but it's still very **high gearing**. Refer to Figures 12.1, 12.2 and 12.3 to see how the position worked out. Note the high profit, due to the extreme gearing involved, that was earned – during this period in the corn versus wheat spread position a result of buying the strength and selling the weakness.

Another aspect to this buy strength and sell weakness strategy is a tendency of many futures bull markets to experience a so-called **price inversion**, also called an inverted market, in which nearby futures gain in price relative to the distant months of the same commodity, and ultimately sell at premiums to the distant markets. This could be due to a tightness, or to a perceived tightness, in **spot** (nearby) supplies. Traders should watch these spread differences carefully, because an inversion of the normal relationship between nearby and distant futures (on a closing price basis) could help confirm a bull market. In fact, I

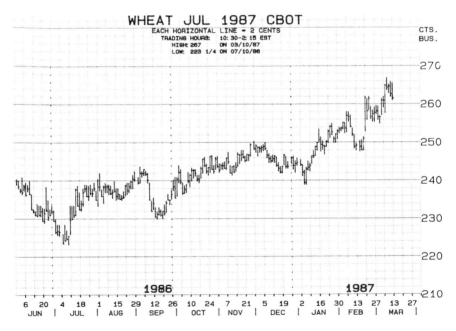

Figure 12.2 July 1987 Wheat. You buy the strength (wheat) and sell the weakness (corn). This is the type of situation that many professional operators seek; it has good profit potential, reasonable risk, and low margin. Opportunities like this appear every year—and the trader should be alert to the chance to buy the strength and sell the weakness. For entry timing, you can take signals from whichever technical or trading system you have confidence in and time each leg on the basis of these signals.

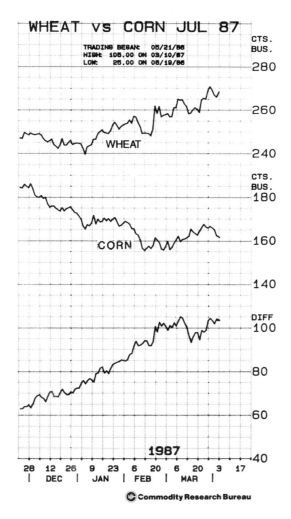

Figure 12.3 July 1987 Wheat versus Corn Spread Chart. As an alternative method of timing spread (buy strength versus sell weakness) trades, you can use spread charts. These charts are available for a broad selection of related markets or two different futures in the same market. You can enter and liquidate positions on the basis of price differences. As an example, let's assume you put on long wheat versus short corn at wheat 70 cents over corn, and the current difference has widened to 1.00 over (you have a 30 cent profit on the position). If you want to stop out if the difference narrowed to, say 90 cents, you would enter the following order. "Buy (quantity) corn and sell (quantity) wheat at 90 cents stop, premium on the wheat." With this order, you would be locking in your profit at 20 cents, less breakage and commissions.

generally add an additional 25% to 50% to any long position I am carrying following such a price inversion.

One other aspect of these so-called spreads, particularly in currency or futures markets, is a tendency among some traders to **straddle up** to avoid taking a loss. Assume for example, you are long May silver with a big loss on the position, and the market is trending down. Rather than take the loss by selling the May silver, some traders would sell July silver instead, effectively locking in the loss at that point. This is not a good idea. This act doesn't prevent the loss; it merely postpones it and the losing position still has to be dealt with in **unwinding** one of the 'legs' of the spread. A more logical strategy is to take the loss, by closing out the original position; then watch the market from an unbiased, sidelines position and re-enter either long or short when the trading indicators provide an objective entry signal.

In summary, it doesn't much matter how you label the basic strategy: hold the profitable position and close out the losing position, or buy the strength and sell the weakness. What is important is that you are aware of it, identify the strong versus weak markets and apply this strategy in a consistent and disciplined manner.

13 Larry Hite: The Billion Dollar Fund Manager

It was mid-summer in 1992. I was driving through New York's Lincoln Tunnel, which connects New York City to New Jersey, passing underneath the venerable Hudson River. The fact that I was driving to New Jersey wasn't very surprising, but the fact that I was doing it in midday, during market hours, was. People who know me, know that it is almost impossible to pry me away from my desk and trading monitor during market hours. So, why the exception?

I was on my way to have lunch with someone whom I've known for some 20 years, since the first time he called on me in my office at 25 Broad Street, in the heart of the Wall Street district. A former stage magician and rock star promoter and a most likeable person, he had a simple proposition for me. He wanted to set up a computerized commodity trading system and then establish a series of futures funds which he would manage and market throughout the world. He wanted to know if I would be willing to join him in this venture?

I briefly took stock in my situation. At the time, I had been in Wall Street for 16 years and for the past eight years, had owned and operated my own commodity brokerage. Not a very large firm, but it had a good reputation, was profitable and, most important, it was mine. I was a member of five commodity exchanges and my firm was a clearing member of the New York Mercantile Exchange. So far, his proposition sounded fine. I had plenty of room in my office and could easily set him and his colleagues up in private offices with whatever equipment they might require. But, there was one problem, and it concerned the 'timing' of this situation.

I had just closed out huge long positions in copper and wheat which I had been nurturing and suffering through for the previous eight months, and on which my clients and I had realized a profit of several million dollars. Perhaps not huge by today's standards, but quite respectable for the early 1970s. I had already determined that, having been in the front line 'trenches' of high stakes speculation for so many years, the time was right for me to close my firm and retire. I was about to relocate to a large four-storey villa at Evian, France, on the shores of the Lake Geneva, which I had purchased the previous year. In fact, I had already informed my clients of the closure, had been sending them back their substantial profits from our trading activities and had informed my staff of the situation. Regretfully, I concluded that it just wasn't possible to turn back and that I would have to inform Larry Hite, of my decision. He went on to become one of the largest commodity fund managers in the world.

There I was, on the way to spend a quiet afternoon with an old friend, looking forward to a nice luncheon, plenty of reminiscing and discussion of future plans. People like Larry Hite always seem to have one eye on the present and one on the future. They're generally too busy to dwell on the past for very long. So, what about this Larry Hite; the billion dollar fund manager?

First of all, he admitted that he doesn't consider himself a very good commodity trader, to which I replied that he could have fooled a lot of people, myself included. His surprising response: he isn't primarily in the commodity business; he considers himself in the 'good bets' business. He said that, when he looks at trading opportunities, he doesn't really see markets and positions. Instead, he sees probabilities, risks and rewards. He notes that the strategy of investing, which includes money management and risk control, is as important, if not more so, than the actual technical aspects of trading. In fact, this is the thesis which underlies much of this book and it's good to see a world class fund manager in complete agreement.

This is what Hite had to say about his development as a fund manager:

> 'I began to devote my resources to developing an unemotional, risk averse quantitative approach to the markets. Price data was subjected to rigorous computer testing to determine if they were recurrent statistical events. If so, then the events were subjected to further testing using strict risk parameters to determine if such a disciplined methodology could be consistently profitable.
>
> I discovered that, yes, I could risk a very small part of the farm, and make above-average returns with reasonable consistency. Yes, I could totally avoid any interpretations of chart patterns or underlying supply and demand factors that impact a particular market, and my returns would not suffer. And yes, I could diversify into many markets, remain extremely disciplined, and still show an appealing return on investment.

I considered my strategy to be a real accomplishment because it has a trading plan that suited my personality and my wallet; disciplined, quantitative and profitable. In short, with the assistance of a statistician and a programmer, I have developed a set of mathematically proven rules that have worked for me.'

Here is what Hite had to say about the 'good bets business':

'I consider myself to be in the good bets business. That is, through the use of a computer, we search for good bets and try to play only good bets. If the bet does not meet our standards, we throw it out, even if it is something that someone else might jump at. This is analogous to actuarial work. Essentially, what I did was to take a highly charged, exhilarating profession and turn it into an actuarial process – something that would appeal to anyone who finds accounting too exciting. I de-emotionalized markets and trading and reduced them to a probability study.'

On trading being 'Zen-like':

'For me, this is a very Zen-like business, and your most valuable tool is yourself. There is a Japanese book about sword fighting whose premise is this: when you get into a sword fight, immediately assume that you're dead so you won't have to worry about being killed. Then, all you have to worry about is making the appropriate moves.

Once you figure out the right action, assemble the means to implement it correctly and then proceed. That is what a good trader does. He or she sets out a programme either through the use of a computer or through some other method to achieve a designated objective. In my case, I thought that de-emotionalizing the markets was the right way to approach the idea of consistent returns. If that is not exciting enough for some people in the business, then so be it. I don't trade for excitement; I trade for profits.'

And on limiting risk:

'It boils down to a de-emotionalized, risk management game for both the big trader and the small speculator. Although we are sometimes involved in as many as 50 markets at any given time, we have a set risk parameter, or stop level, in every one of these 50 markets. Beyond that, we use a maximum percentage draw-down, which relates risk on each position to total equity. That is, we limit the risk on each position in our portfolio to one percent of the account's total equity, based on closing prices. Any time that the loss on any position, as of the close, equals one percent (or more) of total equity, we liquidate that position the following morning.'

In our conversation, I discussed with Larry Hite his strategy for implementing a maximum risk of one percent of the account's equity on each position. I pointed out that, while it was easy to limit losses to within one percent when dealing with accounts in the multi-million dollar category, it would be more difficult for the smaller investor for whom the one percent limitation would obviously be too close. For instance, a one percent limit on an account with US$30,000 would only be US$300, and this would be so close as to stop the trader out recurrently just on the 'noise' from the floor traders' scalping activities.

Hite acknowledged that the one percent limitation would be too restrictive for smaller accounts. Nevertheless, he felt that the general strategy of this approach to risk control was valid. He would, on a smaller account, bump up the risk limitation to approximately two percent of capital. This would still adhere to the general strategy of risk control, but would allow the smaller trader additional leeway. Obviously though, risking more than the recommended one percent limit does make the overall operation more risky, and behoves each trader to exercise even more vigilance to avoid overtrading and other inappropriate tactics.

14 Creating and Using a Technical Trading System

The most critical and the most expensive loss is the loss of confidence. The key to successful is trading begins with the self-confidence to know that; you do have the ability to trade, you can unlearn bad habits and you can learn, with some guidance, to operate successfully.

There are a number of factors underlying a successful and profitable outcome in your speculative operations and we have discussed most of them. This chapter however, focuses on creating and using a technical trading system which, if used in conjunction with sound money management and consistent risk control, should help place you in the 'winners' circle.'

There are an infinite number of trading systems and trading approaches. If you ask nine different for the preferred trading system, you'll get ten different answers, if not more. Over the past 30 or more years, I can't claim to have studied all the trading systems available, but I can categorically say that I have studied many of them. Here are just some of the reputable technical studies people use:

Accumulation/Distribution	Moving Averages, Simple
Average True Range (ATR)	On Balance Volume
Bollinger Bands	Oscillator (MACD)
Commodity Channel Index	Parabolic Stop
Directional Movement Index	Relative Strength Index
Exponential Averages	Stochastics
Keltner Channel	Support and Resistance
Momentum	Volatility Stop
Moving Averages, Exponential	Volume
	Williams %R

The list is virtually endless, and new formulae and indicators are being developed all the time.

My approach to technical analysis can best be summed up by the KIS approach. KIS, as many people know, means keep it simple. In my trading room in Hong Kong, I had spent weeks inspecting and evaluating the computerized technical systems of various data vendors, before finally selecting Telerate as my preferred system. Although I was familiar with and had used most of the available indicators, adhering to the basic KIS method, I only needed some very rudimentary indicators in my work. Telerate obligingly set up a system to suit my personal needs and strategies.

Perhaps some traders believe that, 'more is better,' but for me, 'better is better.' In Wall Street, there is a saying, 'if it's not broke, don't try to fix it.' The method that I have settled on is very definitely 'not broke.' In fact, it works very well for me, so I was absolutely determined to stick with it. There is of course, no perfect or 'right' system. Whatever works for you and is comfortable to use, is the 'right system,' for you. Before describing my 'right' system, allow me to digress briefly and describe some of the various approaches to systems analysis and how to use each of them.

Moving averages

Moving averages are one of the most versatile and widely used of all technical indicators. They are essentially a trend following tool used to signal trend reversals.

- Buy when the faster average crosses above the slower average. This signals an up trend.
- Sell when the faster average crosses below the slower average. This signals a down trend.

Directional movement

The Directional Movement Index (DMI) is a powerful trend-following indicator that tends to give relatively few, but reliable signals. The DMI consists of three components: ADXR, + DI and − DI.

The DMI also measures the directionality of a market, on a scale of 0 to 100. Trade those markets with a higher (above 25/30) ADX. The slope of the ADXR is also important, as a rising ADXR line is consistent with a trending market, while a declining ADXR suggests a non-trending market.

Trending: ADXR > 25/30 or rising 3 points in 1 week.
Non-trending: ADXR < 25/30 and momentum is negative.

ADXR declining from over 35 to under 30 = going from trending to non-trending.

ADXR rising from under 30 to over 35 = going from non-trending to trending.

Buy = up index (+ DI) crosses above the down index (− DI).
Sell = down index (− DI) crosses above the up index (+ DI).

Trade only those markets with an ADXR above 25/30.

Stop out positions using the 'Extreme Point Rule'
On the day that + DI and − DI cross, use the extreme point made that day, as the **Reversal Point**.

1. If you just went long, the reversal stop point is the low made on the day of the crossing.
2. If you just went short, the reversal stop point is the high made on the day of the crossing.
3. Continue to hold this position and the stop, until you are stopped out, even if the lines have crossed.

Additional trading strategy and directional movement
In strong uptrending moves, the + DI and the ADXR turn up early and move higher, with the + DI generally holding above the ADXR. A high-probability signal that the uptrend has stalled or ended is generated when the ADXR line crosses above the + DI, and then turns down. This signal commonly occurs on the day of the trend change or slightly before. It rarely takes more than a few days past a true trend shift to see the ADXR turn down. A warning that a top may be near is often signalled when the + DI stalls and turns down from a high level.

Stochastics

Stochastics determine where the most recent closing price is in relation to the price range for a given time period. Two lines are plotted:

- %K = the faster of the two moving lines.
- %D = the average of %K (the slower moving line).

How to use stochastics
Watch for divergence between the %D line and the price.

- %D should be in the overbought zone (above 80) for a sell.
- %D should be in the oversold zone (below 20) for a buy.

When divergence occurs, the trigger is %K crossing %D.

- Buy signal. When both lines decline into the 20–30 range (or lower) and then %K turns up and crosses above %D within that range.
- Sell signal. When both lines advance into the 70–80 range (or higher) and then %K turns down and crosses below %D within that range.

Bollinger bands

One of the most useful technical concepts developed in recent years is that of trading bands, which are lines drawn at a fixed interval around a moving average. They are widely used to determine overbought and oversold levels.

Bollinger bands are bands that vary in distance from the moving average as a function of the market's volatility. A moving standard deviation is calculated and placed above and below a simple moving average. A 20 period moving average is generally recommended (the central band on Ensign is 21-day moving average).

How to use Bollinger bands

Sharp moves tend to occur after the bands tighten towards the moving average in the centre. A price move outside the bands calls for a continuation of the trend, not an end to it. Bottoms (or tops) made outside the bands followed by bottoms (or tops) made inside the bands call for reversals in the trend. A move originating in one band tends to go all the way to the other band. This observation is useful for projecting targets to moves early on. An experienced analyst suggests that one should start reducing positions when the price goes well beyond both bands.

Relative strength index (RSI)

Relative strength is a ratio of the average of up nets and the average of down nets. This is a popular indicator used to measure overbought and oversold conditions and can be a particularly useful indicator.

How to use RSI

Movements above 70 are considered overbought, while movements below 30 are considered oversold. Watch for the divergence between RSI and price (see Method 1).

- Method 1
  Buy when prices diverge lower and RSI is rising.
  Sell when prices diverge higher and RSI is falling.

For example: RSI goes over 60–70 and prices make a new high, but RSI does not. Topping signal is confirmed when RSI goes below previous low. Bottoming signal is reverse.
- Method 2 (works best in trending markets.)
Buy when RSI crosses above the 50% RSI line.
Sell when RSI crosses below the 50% RSI line.

Look for RSI signals to be confirmed by dual moving average signals.

Everywhere I go, and in virtually every conference or seminar at which I speak, investors seem to be preoccupied by technical trading systems. Here is a commentary about speculation and trading systems that I recently encountered.

'The reader ought to thoroughly understand, however, that there is no royal road to speculation. Given all the conditions of the problem, profits could be ciphered out with the accuracy of a mathematical demonstration. But the unknown quantities are the stumbling blocks of system mongers. Successful operators cannot explain, even to themselves, yet they know when a stock is a good purchase, and when its price is running too high.

How easy it would be to fill a book with these figures! The charts teem with them. There is not a stock . . . which does not indicate alternations of hope and fear in wide percentages and with unbounded opportunities for speculators to buy with confidence of profit. Brokers tell us that one in a hundred buy in this manner; the other ninety-nine mean to do so. They make their calculations, add up and subtract . . . try this system and that theory . . . and come forth from their ventures shorn of all their golden fleece.'

Do these words sound familiar to you? Have you read them in some financial book or market advisory? Well, it's extremely unlikely that you actually read this recently, because it was written by a James K. Medbury in 1870, over 120 years ago.

Well, if traders were experimenting with trading systems back in the last century, they are doing more so than ever in the current one. In fact, it may be true that virtually every serious trader has, at one time or another, experimented with some type of trading system to improve the timing of trade entries, to keep himself in a profitable position longer or to exit a losing trade sooner. All three of these objectives are important and financial success depends on the operator being able to pursue and attain these objectives with maximum consistency.

The universal appeal of a good trend-following system is that, by definition, it should be possible to establish a position in the direction of the trend reasonably near the onset of the move. (Early trend identification depends primarily on the sensitivity of the selected indicators.) The epitome of a good system (a long-term system, in this instance) is that it should tend to keep you in the position so long as the market continues to move favourably, and to stop you out, possibly reversing as well, when the trend reverses. The problem here lies in the phrase, 'tends to keep you in the position,' because as all systems traders have discovered, it is frustratingly difficult to fine tune your stops to stay aboard so long as the market is moving favourably, but (and this is the key 'but') to stop out and possibly reverse at the propitious moment. In the real world of tension-filled, trading, stop placememt, which can at best be a tenuous and imperfect art, will be the key to effective trend trading. It is likely that the stop will either be too close, and you will keep getting stopped out and shipsawed on minor technical corrections; or too far, and you will end up taking huge and untenable losses or else giving back most of your paper profits when the trend reverses. The solution to the problem of fine tuning your stops is probably the most difficult part of successful systems design and is the area that receives the maximum focus in new technical research.

Another problem with trend following systems is that, during periods of broad, sideways price movement, and unfortunately these are more prevalent than are established, dynamic trends, the systems follower is frequently buying on rallies and selling on reactions. These whipsaw losses are, regrettably an inevitable part of trend-following systems trading. The operator needs the patience and financial stamina to sit through a succession of whipsaw losses while waiting for the big move that will provide the big profits. Having the requisite staying power and discipline isn't easy, but my experience has been that, assuming you have a viable and proven trend-following approach, you will do better sticking with it and following it to the letter than trying to second-guess and continually over-ruling it in the quest for 'improved' performance.

On the subject of over-ruling one's proven trading system, there have been many examples, particularly over the last five years. A number of previously successful world-class traders, with consistent long-term system strategies, have abandoned their proven methods in favour of *ad hoc*, discretionary trading and have met with disappointing results. In nearly all cases, these operators have acknowledged the error of abandoning a proven technical system. A more detailed discussion of Trading Systems in general can be found in Chapter 15.

15 Trading Systems: Kroll's Suggested Method

As discussed earlier, out of all the diverse technical methods utilized in trading systems, I have opted for the KIS approach, primarily using moving averages crossover methods. As trading systems go, the moving averages approach is the oldest and most basic of all analysis methods. In its simplest form, a moving average (MA) is the sum of 'x' consecutive closes divided by 'x'. For example, you would obtain a ten-day simple moving averages (SMA) by adding the closing prices for the previous ten days and dividing the sum by ten. Perhaps the most popular SMA combinations are the 5-versus-20-day, and the 4-versus-9-versus-18-day. The 'versus' comes into the picture because systems traders have discovered through years of trial and error and testing, that a 'crossover' technique captures the maximum advantage of a MA trading system.

There are, essentially, two ways to play MA systems, and they can amaze traders by frequently outperforming much more complicated and elaborate systems. In a simple, basic system, where you use, for example, a 12-day SMA, you would buy when the closing price goes above the 12-day SMA, and would sell when the closing price goes below the 12-day SMA. This simple system, however, offers less flexibility and probably inferior performance than the second approach, which uses a dual (or even a triple) crossover, for instance a 5-versus-20-day crossover system. You would buy when the short-term line (the 5-day SMA) crosses above the long-term line (the 20-day SMA), and liquidate long and possibly go short as well, when the opposite occurs.

Serious systems traders tend to get considerably more involved with moving averages. Some use so-called **weighted moving averages** which give greater weight to recent than to older price action, while other operators use exponentially smoothed moving averages, which may incorporate a potentially infinitely smoothed time span via more complex calculations. Such approaches clearly require the use of a personal computer with customized software, where all calculations can be done at lightning speed.

For any moving averages strategy, regardless of its complexity, the critical question concerns the number of days of the analysis and whether it should be optimized (tailored) for each distinct commodity. In this regard, some of the best technical research has been by American analysts Frank Hochheimer and Dave Barker. I should point out that, notwithstanding their excellent research, these studies were done many years ago and should not be depended on today, as markets and overall volatility have changed. Nevertheless, I include this research to indicate how the studies can be done, and as a starting point for modern research.

Hochheimer tested a broad array of moving averages, from 3 to 70 days, on each of 13 different futures for the 1970–1976 period. His results showed that there was not one 'best' universal combination. His best combinations (closing price going through a SMA) which projected best overall profits were:

	Best average (days)	Cumulative profit loss (US$)	Number of trades	Number of profits	Number of losses	Ratio profits/ total trades
Silver	19	42,920 +	1,393	429	964	.308
Pork bellies	19	97,925 +	774	281	493	.363
Corn	43	24,646 +	565	126	439	.223
Cocoa	54	87,957 +	600	157	443	.262
Soybeans	55	222,195 +	728	151	577	.207
Copper	59	165,143 +	432	158	274	.366
Sugar	60	270,402 +	492	99	393	.201

Figure 15.1 Frank Hochheimer's testing of "best-combination" moving average calculations.

It should be noted that these are purely hypothetical trades done on the basis of an after-the-fact calculation. Clearly, real time results are unlikely to show such profits. Also, note the low ratio of profits to total trades, from .201 to .366; quite typical of systems and formula trading.

For those traders interested in going beyond the simple closing price versus a single moving average, the dual moving average crossover would be the next step. With this technique, you calculate both a short-term and a long-term moving average, for example an 8-versus-35-day average. You buy when the 8-day crosses above the 35-day, and you sell when the reverse occurs. Here again, Hochheimer did some excellent research in the testing of optimum crossover periods, using 20 different combinations for the years 1970–1979. Some of his optimum combinations are:

- Silver   13 versus 26 days
- Pork bellies   25 versus 46 days
- Corn   12 versus 48 days
- Cocoa   14 versus 47 days
- Soybeans   20 versus 45 days
- Coppper   17 versus 32 days
- Sugar   6 versus 50 days

Dave Barker also did some fine work in systems testing. He tested the 5-versus-20-day dual MA crossover system (without optimization) versus an optimized dual MA crossover system for the 1975–1980 period. Not surprisingly, the optimized version consistently outperformed the straight 5-versus-20-day version. Here is a partial list of Barker's best combinations:

- Silver   16 versus 25 days
- Pork bellies   13 versus 55 days
- Corn   14 versus 67 days
- Cocoa   14 versus 38 days
- Soybeans   23 versus 41 days
- Copper   4 versus 20 days
- Sugar   14 versus 64 days

It is particularly interesting to note the close correlation between some of Hochheimer's and Barker's optimized crossover combinations.

For those operators who wish to pursue moving averages crossover trading further, here is a description of two trading systems, one long-term and the other short-term, that have been shown to work well in 1992 and 1993.

Long-term system

Either of the following combinations:

- Close versus 5-day EMA versus 8-day EMA.
- Close versus 7-days SMA versus 50-day SMA.

Where: SMA = Simple Moving Averages and
      EMA = Exponential Moving Average

- Buy signal: the first time that the close plus both MA's line up positive, Buy tomorrow on stop at high of today plus 3 ticks.

- Sell signal: the first time that the close plus both MA's line up negative, Sell tomorrow on stop at low of today minus 3 ticks.
- Exiting a market: use money management stop of US$1,500.

It should be noted that this is a long-term system which utilizes loose stops.

Short-term system

Use 60 minute (hourly) bar charts. (For this analysis, you will require an on-line intra-day technical analysis system.) Trades are made on the close or next day's opening. Avoid taking trades based on intra-day signals. Watch the following indicators: close price, 7-day SMA and 50-day SMA.

- Long entry: if you get a bullish close versus 7-SMA versus 50-SMA line-up on 60-minute chart, buy tomorrow on stop at high of today plus 3 ticks.
- Short entry: if you get a bearish close versus 7-SMA versus 50-SMA line-up on 60-minute chart, sell tomorrow on stop at low of today minus 3 ticks.
- Exiting a market: initial stop: US$600.00. Advance stop by US$300 when you have a US$400 profit. Move stop to break even after US$800 profit. Do not change this stop.

As you can readily see, one of the virtues of a computerized trading system is that it is quite specific and exact. Another significant feature is that it suffers no bias for the long side of each market, as the majority of speculators do. All signals are derived from the mathematics within the system.

In essence, it boils down to this. A trading system is a tool, and like most tools, there are quality ones and mediocre ones. No system can be the 'ultimate answer' to consistent profits and at best must be combined with good market strategy, money management and viable risk control. There are still plenty of successful traders who wouldn't know the difference between a data disk and a slipped disk. However, in the hands of an objective and disciplined operator, the 'right' system can be a significant aid for successful trading. But, and here comes the big 'but' again, its benefit will be proportional to the patience and discipline with which the operator applies the system.

Chapters 14 and 15 should have provided you with a realistic, understandable introduction to systems trading. For a more detailed study, which is outside the scope of this book, refer to other works completely devoted to computer systems trading.

16 The Intricacies of Order Entry Procedures

The aspect of the Merrill Lynch training programme I enjoyed the least back in my trainee days, was the time devoted to learning the correct entry of orders. It seems like we spent hours on the technicalities of entering all manner of orders and then practising them over and over – from the point of view of the client, the account executive and the dealer.

But, shortly after 'graduating' from the training programme and being assigned as an account executive in one of Merrill Lynch's midtown Manhattan offices, I began to realize how important this subject is. I silently thanked whoever had the good sense to include such rigorous coverage in the training programme.

Over the intervening years, I have been dismayed at how little most investors and traders really know about order entry procedures, including many experienced professional. Investors should be proficient in entering orders and receiving confirmations for two reasons:

1. Incorrect or faulty order entry procedure can result in costly errors. Brokerage firms often record all order confirmations and, in the event of a disputed error, will play back the tape. If you made the error, you pay to correct it. It's as simple as that, and ignorance of the correct procedure is no defense.

Besides, even if the dealer commits the error and, you are sharp enough to catch it before it becomes too expensive to fix, you'd have scored some points with the firm and have made some valuable friends.

2. Knowing the correct order entry procedure for all types of orders will facilitate your trading and, will allow you the flexibility to structure a variety of tactical plays that are denied to traders who know just the simple, basic type of orders.

Whatever the order, your first priority is to speak slowly and distinctly. Concentrate on your order and what you are actually saying. Many erros have been committed by people wanting to sell, but after a diversion and reading the word 'buy' on another ticket, mistakenly enter the order as a buy. Furthermore, it is imperative that the account executive or dealer (order clerk) repeat the order back to you. There can be no exception to this. What if the dealer takes your order and hangs up without repeating it? Call him back and politely ask him to repeat the order. Also, when he calls you back with the report of your fill, you should repeat it to him too.

Here are the components that make up all orders:

1. Buy or Sell
The first part of any order is to **buy** or **sell**. Always repeat this part of the order, for example: 'buy five May sugar at the market. Buy it.' It may sound superfluous and wordy, but it helps ensure that the other party knows whether you want to buy or sell.

2. Quantity
Futures trades are specified in number of contracts, with one exception; grains, where you would specify the number of bushels. Since one grain contract is for 5,000 bushels, if you want to buy one contract of corn, for example, you would order, 'buy 5,000 bushels of (month) corn.' This would also apply to orders for oats, soybeans and wheat. An order for twenty contracts would be stated as, '100,000 bushels.'

3. Delivery Month
For commodity futures, be clear about which contract month you want to trade in, such as 'May corn,' 'July wheat,' or 'December cocoa.' Obviously, this does not apply to stock orders.

4. Commodity
This is quite straightforward, but some commodities may sound nearly alike, such as 'cotton' and 'copper,' so it is necessary to speak clearly and distinctly. Also, if the commodity is traded on more than one exchange, that exchange must be specified. For example, gold is traded on various exchanges, so you must specify which one.

5. Price
Price can have a number of variables:
   (a) **Market order** is exactly what it sounds like: the floor broker will fill your order at the best price he can, as quickly as possible. You should not have any illusions about the floor broker watching the market and waiting around to try and get you a better fill. His job is to fill the order and get the report back to you quickly and accurately. Under normal circum-

stances he will buy at the 'offer' or sell at the 'bid.' If you want to give the broker some discretion in filling your market order (and it's up to him if he wants to take that discretion), you can enter it on a 'not held,' or 'take your time' basis. For example, your order can be entered as, 'Sell 50 March copper at the market, not held.' This type of designation is usually entered with larger orders where you may not want to buy at the offer or sell at the bid, especially if the market is thin. With such larger orders, it helps to talk to the floor broker beforehand (outside trading hours preferably) to be sure you both understand what to do.

(b) With a **limit order**, you don't want to sell at the then-current market price. Instead, you will specify your price limit above which you do not want to buy, or below which you do not want to sell. A limit order to buy will be placed below the market; a limit order to sell will be placed above the market. It isn't necessary to accompany a limit order with the designation, 'or better.' All limit orders are understood to be 'or better.' That is, the broker will always try to get a better price for you, if he can.

(c) A **stop order**, in its basic terms, is an order to buy if the price hits a specified level above the market, or an order to sell if the price hits a specified price below the market.

Let's say the trend in sugar is up, and you are long three contracts of March sugar from lower levels. The current price is 7.11 cents per pound and you want to add to your long position only if the market can surpass the 7.25 level, against which it has failed on several occasions. In such a case, you might enter the following order: 'buy two March sugar at 7.27 stop.' This order will become a market order to buy if the price trades at or above, or is bid at or above, 7.27 (your stop price). You can also enter a 'stop on close' order, which kicks in as a market order if the market closes at or above your buy stop price, or at or below your sell stop price. A word of caution here: your 'stop on close' order might be filled far beyond your specified stop price.

A sell stop, on the other hand, is a resting order to sell at a price below the market. It becomes a market order if the price trades at or below, or is offered at or below, your stop price. The same holds true for sell stop 'on close.'

In volatile markets, especially if there is an accumulation of stop orders at or around a particular price, it's not unusual for stop orders to be filled beyond (at a worse price) the specified stop price.

As an alternative to a straight stop order, you can enter a stoplimit order (check with your broker; some brokers or exchanges will not accept stoplimit orders). Whereas a stop order becomes a market order if the stop is elected, a stoplimit order becomes a limit order if its stop is elected. This has both an advantage and a disadvantage. While it ensures you do not get filled at worse than your limit price, you may miss being filled if the market moves beyond your limit before the floor broker can act.

(d) **One cancels the other (OCO)** involves two related orders; whichever is filled first, the other is cancelled. For example, if August gold is trading in a range between 384.50 and 388.50, you might enter the following order: Buy two August gold at 389.50 stop or sell two August gold at 383.50 stop, one cancels the other.

(e) **Market if touched (MIT)** is a limit order that becomes a market order if your MIT price is touched. For example, May soybeans are trading at 5.49 per bushel and you want to go long if the price declines to 5.42. You don't want to take a chance of missing the market if the price ticks at 5.42 and then abruptly rises. Your order could read: 'Buy 10M May soybeans at 5.42 MIT.' Of course, your risk is that you may pay a bit higher for the fill, but at least you are guaranteed of a fill on even a single tick at your MIT price.

(f) **When done** is a contingent order that says, 'after you have filled this order, please enter the following order.' For example, 'sell five December silver at 536.00; when done, enter an open stop at 545.00.' We usually use the term 'EOS,' which stands for 'enter open stop.' You must check with your broker to see if he accepts contingent orders because some exchanges will not accept them.

6. Time Duration

Unless you specify otherwise, all orders are understood to be day orders—that is, if an order has not been filled during that session, it expires. If you want an order to remain in force beyond the day of entry, you must specify it when you enter.

You can enter a 'good till cancelled' (open) order, which remains in force until it is either filled or cancelled. Alternatively, your order can be 'good through a specified date,' such as, 'buy two July sugar at 11.55, good through September 30.' In all open or good through a specified date orders, you are responsible for cancelling them when required, such as when you liquidate the position with another order but still have the previous order in force.

7. Spreads

A spread order, also called a 'switch' or a 'straddle,' is quite a common order. It refers to the simultaneous purchase and sale of two delivery months of the same commodity, or two different but related commodities. There are three reasons why traders use spread orders:

(a) You are taking a speculative position based on an analysis that one 'leg' of the spread (your buy side) will advance relative to the other 'leg' (your sell side).

(b) Your nearby futures position is approaching delivery and you want to 'roll' it forward into a more distant futures position.

(c) The third, and regrettably, quite common spread tactic is to spread a losing position rather than liquidating it, with the rationale that you do not want to take the loss. This is a distinctly bad idea. It just compounds your problem and adds to the loss. My advice is never straddle to avoid closing out a position with a loss.

One final suggestion when shifting a position forward (rollover): unless you are a very experienced short-term trader, you are better off giving the rollover order to the broker as a spread and letting him fill it that way. This will ensure that you don't miss a market by closing one 'leg' and then missing the market on your new 'leg.'

8. Cancelling Orders

You must be very precise whenever you cancel an order. You start by telling the broker whether you have a 'straight cancel' or a 'cancel and replace.' The straight cancel is easy: 'cancel to buy ten July Hang Seng at 8,640.' If, on the other hand, you are entering a cancel and replace, you start by saying, 'I have a cancel and replace for you.' Then you give him the order: 'sell five July sugar at the market, cancel to sell five at 12.35 stop open.'

9. Errors

What do you do if, despite your best precautions, you discover you made an error on an order? You should immediately phone your broker or the dealer and inform him. At this stage, it's more important to deal with the error than to argue who caused it. You can determine the responsibility later.

First, be sure you and the broker or dealer agree on what actually happened. Did you buy or sell, which month of what future, and at what price? Then, you make a quick decision on whether you are willing to take the fill. For example, you may have intended to buy March sugar but the broker bought the same quantity of May. If it's a new (opening) position, you may be willing to accept the long May; however, if you are covering a March short position, then you need a fill in March and not May.

In summary, if you can't use the 'error' trade, get out of it immediately. Don't sit back and try to 'play' the error. You may get lucky and work out of it successfully. But, more likely than not you'll compound the error and end up with a bigger loss than the original one. Keep this maxim in mind: 'the first loss is usually the cheapest.'

Overview of Trends and Price Levels

1. Regarding Trends
    (a) A market should not be considered bullish or bearish, so you should avoid taking any bullish or bearish view of any market.
    (b) Simply take the pictures based on the technical indicators:
        (i) If the technical indicators point up, be long.
        (ii) If the technical indicators point down, be short.
    (c) Livermore said:
        'There is no such thing as the bullish or bearish side of a market; There is only the right side.'

2. Regardubg Oruce Keveks
    (a) A market is never to high to buy or too low to sell.
    (b) Do not go short because a market is too high, or overbought. It will probably go higher.
        Do not go long because a market is too low, or oversold. It will probably go lower.
    (c) Bottom line: Base trades on the objective, proven indicators. Do not make exceptions!

Murphy's Law in Futures Trading

Let us begin with a description of Murphy's Law. It is a tendency for things to happen based on the following; if something can go wrong, it will. Premise a more colourful description is; if you drop a slice of bread with Jam on are side, on your new carpet, it will invariably land jam side down.

Futures traders are not particularly concerned about dropping slices of bread, with or without jam on the carpet. But, we are concerned with implementing successful strategies in our trading operations.

In this regard, Murphy's Law 'tells' us the following; if you want to know, in advance, which trades are likely to be the biggest losers, it is those trades for which you neglect to enter a protective stop, or for which carelessly enter a larger position than you should.

To avoid the adverse effects of these so-called Murphy's Law trades, you should consistently enter protective stops whenever you put on a position and establish the maximum number of contracts to put on for each size account, and not exceed that number under any circumstances.

Murphy's Law can be very amusing under many conditions, but not in connection with real-time commodity trading.

Conclusion: The Market Doesn't Take Prisoners

The seasoned operator has learned from long and costly experience that he is going to encounter good periods, with successful trades and uplifted spires (they generally go together), and bad periods, with a preponderance of losing crudes and negative emotions.

What is required is a good sense of emotional balance and market perspective. He must ride out those good times and not become seduced by sudden success; and must avoid getting carried away (or carried out) during the bad times.

Disappointment and discouragement are two basic human emotions with which the serious commodity trader is well acquainted. He must maintain the self-discipline to overcome discouragement and consistently adhere to objective, systematic methods of futures trading. He must maintain the self-confidence to be able to get through the bad days (or weeks) because that is the only way to make the losses back, with interest, during the next good period.

And, no matter how grin things may appear, there definitely will be a 'next good period' so ling as the operator stays (financially) alive by limiting losses on adverse positions.

Bottom Line

The most damaging loss, and the one to be avoided at all costs, is the loss of confidence and belief in your ability to trade with consistent success — you must avoid that loss at all costs.

17 Epilogue: Kroll Market Strategy for Consistent Profits

I should say, at the outset, that it was never my intention to include the following material in this book. This chapter outlines the actual working strategy that I use in trading for my large managed accounts, individual and institutional. Generally, such information is considered proprietary and extremely confidential. So why did I agree to include it? Well, I've been in this business over 33 years and I've written five books on trading. Wall Street has been good to me for over three decades, and after much consideration, I felt that if this strategy can help other investors, it would be good for me to share it.

However, a few words of explanation are in order. The following strategy is not going to work for everyone and it would be a mistake to consider this a general approach. It is very much an individual and personal approach to trading, and it should be taken that way. Does it work for me? Unequivocally, yes. Will it work for you? Perhaps not, at least in the explicit way it has been presented. It is my hope that serious traders will read and consider this and will refine and adapt the tactics and strategies to their own personal style. Also, the final page details 'Maximum risk per contract,' for futures contracts. Probably, no two traders will agree exactly. Some may find the risk (stop distance) too loose, and others too tight. This is the result of testing, both by computer and by trial and error, and again it seems to work for me. Remember, this is the investment strategy of one person, myself, and it relates to futures trading, although it could easily be amended to include stock trading, as well.

Stanley Kroll trading strategy

- Kroll is a long-term systems trader for profitable positions, tending to remain in profitable trades for at least nine weeks; and

91

a short-term systems trader for adverse positions, tending to remain in adverse trades for less than three weeks.

- He uses a mechanical trading system and generally takes every trade generated by the system, except he may only take a maximum of two currencies (for each client) out of the four that he follows. In general, he will not use discretion, except where markets are extremely volatile, when he will exercise discretion to reject new trades or to make an early exit from existing trades.

  The main advantage of being a systems trader is that, if the system is working properly, in synch with the market, it will produce a constant risk-reward ratio over time.

- He is a diversified money manager, since he follows and trades some 26 different futures contracts, covering all the major US markets, plus the Hong Kong and SIMEX markets.

- He is a technical trader, with robust entry and exit signals being price based. Signals are based on a technical analysis of each market. The signals are not optimized and utilize the same indicators for all markets.

- He is a relatively conservative money manager, utilizing not more than 30% of each account's equity to margin trades. He will typically trade just one to three contracts of each market for accounts up to US$100,000. This avoids excessive leverage and excessive trading. The remaining 70% of capital is invested in **T-Bills** and held in reserve.

- He constructs his portfolios to include the largest number of diverse market groups: currencies, food and fibres, interest rate instruments, the energy complex, grains, meats, metals and Asian markets. Within each group he trades the major contracts, choosing the most active months. In such a broadly diversified portfolio, there is relatively weak correlation between the groups.

- He has no bias between long and short positions. He is mindful when constructing portfolios, to effect a realistic and defensive balance between long and short positions. His basic strategy is to buy (go long) the strength and to sell (go short) the weakness.

- He employs strict risk control limits for each marker. Typically, initial risk, or money management stop, is placed at less than US$1,500 per contract. The precise amount is determined from historical testing to support long-term trading. If stops are too wide, there are unacceptably high losses; if stops are too close, the frequency of trades increases and profit per trade decreases. Hence, stops are set to allow trades time to develop. Stops are entered daily before the markets open and every position will have a stop in force every day. He risks an average of 1% to 2% of the account's equity, (depending on size) on each market position.

- Kroll selectively uses trading stops. Depending on the market and its technical characteristics, he sometimes places stops based on volatility, amount of profit in the trade and time in the trade.

In some markets, which have historically trended well, he may not **trail** (advance) his stops. In such markets, the trading models are deemed to have sufficient sensitivity to respond to trend changes in a timely manner. In general, his stop placement strategy is to allow time and space for long-term trades to develop.

- He does not try to pick tops and bottoms. He is almost always in the market for most of his contracts. Upon entering a with-the-trend position he premises that each position could result in a major move and stays for as much of the move as possible. The stops will 'tell' him when to get out when the market reverses.
- If he gets stopped out prematurely and the following day, the market trend remains the same, he will get back aboard the market in the same trend direction, using his objective entry strategies.
- Generally his entry strategy for new accounts is to wait for new signals. However, if he has a recent entry signal which is showing a loss, he may enter the trade based on the number of days in the trade and the recent market action.

Stanley Kroll
Trading Strategy
Maximum Risk per Contract (March 1994)

		US$	*Points*
1.	Bellies	1,250	312
2.	British Pound	1,500	240
3.	Cocoa	1,000	100
4.	Coffee	1,500	4.00
5.	Copper	1,250	5.00
6.	Corn	750	15.00
7.	Cotton	1,250	250
8.	Crude oil	1,250	125
9.	Deutsch Mark	1,500	120
10.	Euro-Dollar	400	16
11.	Gold	1,500	15.00
12.	Hogs	500	125
13.	Heating oil	1,000	238
14.	Japanese Yen	1,500	120
15.	Silver	1,500	30.00
16.	Soybeans	1,250	25.00
17.	Sugar	750	120
18.	Swiss Franc	1,500	120
19.	T-Note 10 Year	1,500	48
20.	US Bond	1,500	48
21.	Wheat	1,000	20.00
22.	Hang Seng Index (HK)	975	150
23.	Nikkei Index (SGPRE)	960	200

Summary for 23 markets:
  Total risk   US$26,125
  Average risk per contract   US$1,178

18 Postscript: Investment Opportunities in China and Hong Kong for the 1990s

Twenty years ago, it was said that the average Chinese aspired to own a bicycle, a sewing machine and a wrist watch. In the 1980s, to this list was added a colour TV, a refrigerator and other appliances. Now, in the 1990s, it may be difficult to forecast the next national 'wish list,' but it would probably include a video player, stereo system, air conditioning, a cellular phone and, for people of the upper income bracket, an automobile.

How can one describe China economically? The statistics can be difficult to comprehend. It has some of the world's largest manufacturing and service corporations. It is a market of 1.2 billion consumers. It has workforce of 700 million and an economy that is growing by about 13% (contrasting with a growth rate of some 3% in the US). And, it is receiving untold billions of investment dollars pouring in from virtually every corner of the developed world.

Economists forecast that China's economic growth could average some 9% through to the end of this century, as the nation pursues economic reforms. But this growth is by no means guaranteed and the path may not be smooth, as it is likely to be accompanied by rapid inflation, roller-coaster world sentiment and an underdeveloped infrastructure.

Fifteen years ago, China's paramount leader, Deng Xiaoping gave a historic speech that helped trigger an economic revolution. Deng said, simply, 'Poverty is not a characteristic of socialism.' With these words, he launched a move to take China forward and to help bring the modern Chinese society towards what he called, 'the well-to-do society.'

After the decade-long Cultural Revolution, which threw China into virtual chaos and brought the country to the verge of bankruptcy, China's leaders found that the country was largely isolated from world development. The Chinese peoples' living standards were found to be

95

as low as in 1952, when China first started rehabilitating its economy after World War II.

In 1978, the State Statistical Bulletin reported, 'The supply of meat, poultry, feed grains and other foodstuffs is short . . . and cannot meet the increasing demands of the people.' Most foodstuffs and even consumer goods, from bicycles to laundry soap, were rationed. But, by 1992, distribution coupons had been abolished and the per capita output of meat, eggs and feed grains were 25 kilograms, 8 kilograms and an astonishing 380 kilograms respectively; on par with world levels. Deng said that in the reform, 'Some people should be allowed to become well-off earlier.'

His words are now coming true. But the mid 1990s, the economy was growing swiftly, diversifying and gaining confidence. Reform brought great changes to Chinese society and dramatically improved living standards, especially for the more developed regions.

When I was a novice Merrill Lynch account executive, I recall talking with a knowledgeable Wall Streeter about Swiss bankers. I especially remember this statement: 'if you see a Swiss banker jump out of the window, you can follow him. Not only will he have a soft landing, but he'll probably make money on the way down.' Obviously, an exaggeration, but not without a certain modicum of truth. Recently, The Swiss Bank Corporation, one of Switzerland's 'Big Three,' announced a further move into China, through the launch of a representative office in Shanghai, its second on the Chinese mainland. 'It is a clear indication that our bank wants to expand its business there, 'noted a spokesman from the Beijing office of Swiss Bank, in their characteristically taciturn manner.

Well, if the quintessential Swiss banker opts to 'jump' into China, what should we do about it? Should we get more involved in China? And when do we do it? As a long-time Wall Street trader, I have been trained that, before I start talking about profit potential, I consider it appropriate to talk about the risks involved.

- We are only looking at the growth of China over the past 15 years. This is a very short time over which to draw long range inferences.
- Deng, China's paramount leader, is 89 years of age, and there is considerable uncertainty about China's leadership, direction and economic outlook in a post-Deng era.
- There is very little consistent infrastructure in China. Economic corruption and scandals seem to be rampant. While the government seems to have the will to clean things up, one has to question whether it has the experience or the human resources to do the job adequately.

- I have frequently been asked to list the commodity products and the futures markets of China. Aside from the better known and established exchanges, such as Beijing, Shanghai, Shenzhen, Zhengzhou and a new petroleum exchange in Nanjing, one can observe that the majority of exchanges in China seem to have a confusing and uncertain future of their own. Currently, it is estimated that there are more than 100 exchanges and **forward markets** in China and more than 80,000 farmers' markets or trade fairs have burgeoned nationwide.
- Legal enforcement of contracts is generally not up to the standards which many other countries take for granted and which is necessary for the consistent pursuit of serious business objectives.
- Despite serious efforts to rein in inflation and excess slack in the money supply, these impediments to a stable economy and business environment still exist and it is uncertain whether they can be brought under control in the foreseeable future.
- Finally, the world expects certain standards concerning human rights and environmental issues and hopes that China will not rekindle some of its old problems and conditions, with the ensuing consequences of severe social and economic dislocation. But there remains uncertainty regarding its political will in these respects.

China's fledgling commodity industry is in danger of becoming a victim of its own rapid, unregulated expansion. With commodity markets springing up all over the country, the growth is both disorganized and often duplicative. It has taken some five years to set up commodity trading in China. Now, contracts, mainly for grains, other farm produce and edible oils, petroleum and metals are being traded on exchanges in Beijing, Nanjing Shanghai, Shenzhen and Zhengzhou. But in addition to the established exchanges, there is a huge expansion of new futures exchanges which is resulting in multiple markets for the same commodities. There are, reportedly, more than 20 officially ratified wholesale markets and so-called futures exchanges in the country and some 30 more about to open or in the planning stages.

Major Commodity Exchanges In China (January 1994)

Name	Product traded	Year established
Beijing Jinpen Copper Exchange	Copper	1991
Beijing Mercantile Futures Exchange	Commodities	1993
Beijing Petroleum Futures Exchange	Petroleum	1992
Nanjing Petroleum Futures Exchange	Petroleum	1992
Shanghai Metals Exchange	Nonferrous metals	1992
Shenzhen Metals Exchange	Nonferrous metals	1992
Zhengzhou Grain Futures Exchange	Grain	1990

Some local authorities take it for granted that establishing their own futures markets can make the local politicians and entrepreneurs, who are often one and the same people, rich. At the same time, a strong measure of local protectionism is making some regional governments fence off outside products from their areas and, although Beijing has reaffirmed that futures exchanges and companies must be approved by the central government, some local authorities still claim the right to sanction them.

It is difficult to invest directly in Chinese companies because, as of March 1994, only about four dozen companies are allowed to sell special 'B' class shares, established in 1991, to foreigners. Instead, international investors have targeted Hong Kong, whose stock market includes many companies with business ties to China. Investors, including those in search of a 'China play,' have pumped up Hong Kong share prices tremendously in the past two years, notwithstanding the recent market correction. The handful of mutual funds that focus entirely on China have earned shareholders big returns during that period.

While it is not yet a simple proposition to buy and sell in the fledgling stock markets of Shanghai and Shenzhen, there are other ways for foreign investors to participate in the growth of China. This includes several closed-end investment companies and a growing number of open-end funds, with global or Asia-only portfolios that have been buying into China-related stocks. A handful of stocks of Chinese firms have already been listed on the New York Stock Exchange and, as China develops into a more open economic system, additional public offerings are likely both in New York and Hong Kong. In short, at least for now, the logical place for most Western investors to gain exposure to China is through mutual funds.

There is another way for Western investors to participate in this China growth, albeit much more risky and requiring more knowledge and money. China is considering new ways of attracting foreign investment to bail out failing state enterprises, including selling them outright to overseas interests. China would like to have financially strong foreign companies, so called 'white knight enterprises', take over the unhealthy ones. But the problem is, there are far more ailing enterprises than there are healthy ones willing or able to invest in them.

Looking ahead to the 21st century, the real major beneficiaries of China's growth could be companies in Japan, Korea, Hong Kong and Taiwan, that produce high value-added goods, not just simple things like textiles or steel. What China will need, over the long run, is what we can call 'mid-tech' equipment such as efficient power plants, refineries, modern steel mills, electronics factories and automobile plants, and these Asian countries are the ones to supply them.

Conclusions: Hong Kong after 1997

The economic fate of Hong Kong after 1997 is a major question. Let's try to separate the facts and logic from the rumours and speculation. It is not possible to consider the question of Hong Kong after 1997 without also thinking about China. China clearly lacks, and may lack for some time to come, a well organized domestic infrastructure, the rule of law and contracts, free international currency exchange and good communications, both domestically and internationally. In addition, bureaucratic inefficiency and an unacceptable degree of corruption are a fact of life in Chinese affairs.

Accordingly, for much of the world, Hong Kong will continue to serve as the gateway to China and will benefit from further Sino expansion, but with less of the uncertainty and risk of direct China involvement. In effect, if one can develop a good multinational strategy, Hong Kong could be a viable solution to the 'China play' that everyone seeks. Many Hong Kong stocks, particularly in the banking and mid- and-high-tech industries, are very involved with China, and their growth and profitability are linked to the mainland. Clearly, another potential China 'play.' Also, with its proximity and affinity to China, Hong Kong will further benefit from the expansion of the financial, engineering and construction sectors in China. This suggests that sound, well managed land and property development, engineering and construction concerns may benefit as well.

As we approach 1997 the Hong Kong-China border may expand, with Hong Kong enlarging and further developing. This general expansion of Hong Kong could result in additional inflation and, as the population increases, especially with the mainland China influx, Hong Kong could develop additional social problems. At the same time, big infrastructural projects in China will require Hong Kong to supply the additional human resources, both at the top and bottom ends of the labour market.

And finally, the government and administration of Hong Kong may lose some of the efficiency and good order that the pre-1997 British administration provided. Such a loss would further enhance the attractiveness of sound, well managed Hong Kong financial and service-oriented firms in the private sector.

Epilogue to Chapter 18

We have stressed, in Chapter 18, the great uncertainty surrounding the financial markets in China, and the inability of anyone to establish a viable strategy for operating there. To confirm this point is the Reuters article which appeared on 15 June 1994. The article is self-explanatory, and serves to underscore the uncertainty of China's financial markets.

SHANGHAI, 15 June 1994 (Reuters) China plans to turn most of its futures exchanges into wholesale markets in a sweeping crackdown on the infant futures industry, the China Securities News reported.

Wholesale markets will not be allowed to engage in futures business, according to detailed directives issued by the State Council, China's cabinet.

Only a small number of futures exchanges will be allowed to stay in business after strict vetting by the Securities Commission of the State Council. No new futures floors will be approved, the newspaper reported.

The paper said the recently-issued directives called for a 'strick halt to the blind development of the futures market.'

Futures brokerages will be barred from placing orders on overseas markets. They must either offset their present outstanding positions the day before delivery, or take physical delivery, and then remit guarantee funds.

Remaining futures exchanges must conduct most of their businesses in commodities and financial futures and will be strictly controlled.

Index-linked futures trading is banned and until a currency futures regulation is promulgated, currency rate-linked futures are also prohibited, the directives say.

National-level companies with futures brokerages must also be rigorously examined by the Securities Commission and will only be allowed to conduct business with designated overseas futures exchanges and in approved products.

Overseas brokerages acting on behalf of these companies must be authorized by the Commission. The companies must follow China's import and export regulations for physical delivery.

Overseas hedging by designated foreign exchange banks and non-bank financial institutions must be supervised by the State Administration of Exchange Control and the Securities Commission, the directives said.

In principle, foreign invested and joint venture futures brokerages will not be allowed to re-register.

Access to futures markets by state-run enterprises will be strictly controlled and loss-making enterprises will be banned altogether. All futures trading that has not been authorized will be considered illegal. The state will confiscate the equipment and all revenue from illegal operations and will punish, or even prosecute, officials in charge.

In a separate editorial, the China Securities News said that in the past two or three years, more than 40 futures exchanges and 400 brokerages had been set up in China.

The paper gave details of standards that will be applied in approving futures exchanges.

Standard futures contracts must account for more than 90 per cent of their trading and physical delivery must account for less than five percent of volume. In the first four months of this year, their daily turnover must have exceeded 100 million yuan and they must have at least 50 members. In addition,they must be located in major cities.

On Sunday the People's Daily newspaper said that blind speculation in futures had led to huge outflows of capital from China and big losses for the state.

Appendix

LIVE CATTLE

Chicago Mercantile Exchange
Monthly High, Low, Close
Nearest Futures Contract

EACH GRID = .5
CENTS PER LB.

AS OF 03/31/94

CONTRACT SPECIFICATIONS

Exchange
Chicago Mercantile Exchange

Trading Hours
8:45 a.m. to 1:00 p.m. Central Time

Trading Months
February, April, June, August, October, and December

Contract Size
40,000 lb.

Prices Quoted In
Cents per lb.

Minimum Fluctuation
.025 cent

Value of Minimum Fluctuation
$10.00

Maximum Permissible Limit
1-1/2 cents

Value of Maximum Permissible Limit
$600

First Delivery Notice
Last business day, if on Monday, Tuesday, Wednesday, or Thursday, of the month preceding the contract month.

Last Trading Day
Business day immediately preceding the last 5 business days of the contract month.

10 Year Weekly Nearest Future
High: 84.30 (Apr '93 on 3-23-93)
Low: 50.72 (Aug '85 on 7-29-85)

20 Year Monthly Nearest Future
High: 84.30 (Apr '93 on 3-23-93)
Low: 33.75 (Jun '74 on 6-12-74)

Reprinted with permission © 1994 Knight-Ridder Financial
30 South Wacker Drive, Suite 1820, Chicago, Illinois 60606

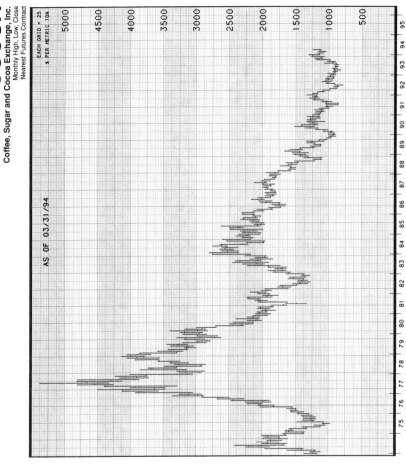

COCOA

Coffee, Sugar and Cocoa Exchange, Inc.
Monthly High, Low, Close
Nearest Futures Contract

AS OF 03/31/94

EACH GRID = 25
$ PER METRIC TON

CONTRACT SPECIFICATIONS

Exchange
New York Coffee, Sugar and Cocoa Exchange

Trading Hours
9:00 a.m. to 2:00 p.m. Eastern Time

Trading Months
March, May, July, September, and December

Contract Size
10 metric tons (22,046 lbs.)

Prices Quoted In
Dollars per metric ton

Minimum Fluctuation
$1.00

Value of Minimum Fluctuation
$10.00

Maximum Permissible Limit
$88.00

Value of Maximum Permissible Limit
$880

First Delivery Notice
7 business days before first day of delivery month.

Last Trading Day
11 business days prior to the last full
business day of the delivery month.

Crop Year
October 1 to September 30

10 Year Weekly Nearest Future
High: 2,747 (Jul '84 on 5-21-84)
Low: 785 (Jul '92 on 6-24-92)

20 Year Monthly Nearest Future
High: 5,379 (Jul '77 on 7-18-77)
Low: 1,028 (May '73 on 5-2-73)

Reprinted with permission © 1994 Knight-Ridder Financial
30 South Wacker Drive, Suite 1820, Chicago, Illinois 60606

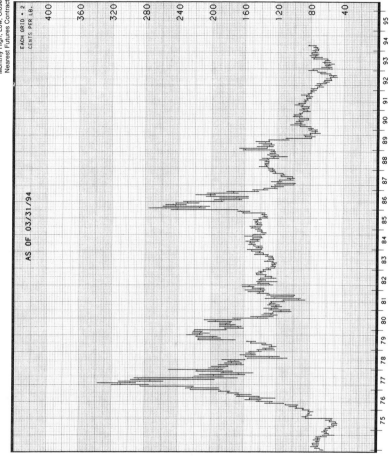

COFFEE

Coffee, Sugar and Cocoa Exchange, Inc.
Monthly High, Low, Close
Nearest Futures Contract

AS OF 03/31/94

EACH GRID = 2
CENTS PER LB.

CONTRACT SPECIFICATIONS

Exchange
New York Coffee, Sugar and Cocoa Exchange

Trading Hours
9:15 a.m. to 1:58 p.m. Eastern Time

Trading Months
March, May, July, September, and December

Contract Size
37,500 lb.

Prices Quoted In
Cents per lb.

Minimum Fluctuation
.05 cent

Value of Minimum Fluctuation
$18.75

Maximum Permissible Limit (variable limit)
6 cents

Value of Maximum Permissible Limit
$2,250

First Delivery Notice
Five business days before the first day of delivery
month.

Last Trading Day
8 business days prior to the last full business day
of the delivery month.

Crop Year
October 1 to September 30

10 Year Weekly Nearest Future
High: 276.00 (Mar '86 on 1-7-86)
Low: 48.10 (Sep '92 on 8-17-92)

20 Year Monthly Nearest Future
High: 337.50 (May '77 on 4-14-77)
Low: 45.25 (May '75 on 4-11-75)

HIGH GRADE
COPPER
Commodity Exchange, Inc.
Monthly High, Low, Close
Nearest Futures Contract

EACH GRID = 1
CENTS PER LB.

AS OF 03/31/94

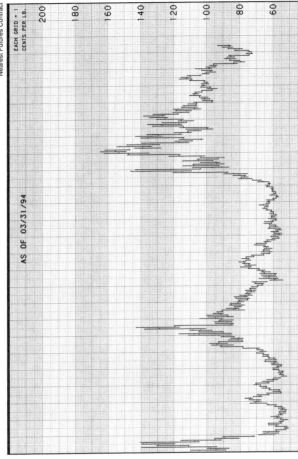

CONTRACT SPECIFICATIONS

Exchange
New York Commodity Exchange, Inc. (COMEX)

Trading Hours
9:25 a.m. to 2:00 p.m. Eastern Time

Trading Months
March, May, July, September, December, and
spot month

Contract Size
25,000 lbs.

Prices Quoted In
Cents per lbs.

Minimum Fluctuation
.05 cents

Value of Minimum Fluctuation
$12.50

Maximum Permissible Limit
None

First Delivery Notice
2nd to last business day of calendar month preceding
month of delivery.

Last Trading Day
The 3rd to the last business day of a maturing delivery
month.

10 Year Weekly Nearest Future
High: 164.75 (Dec '88 on 12-8-88)
Low: 54.70 (Oct '84 on 10-17-84)

20 Year Monthly Nearest Future
High: 164.75 (Dec '88 on 12-8-88)
Low: 50.80 (Jan '75 on 1-20-75)

Reprinted with permission © 1994 Knight-Ridder Financial
30 South Wacker Drive, Suite 1820, Chicago, Illinois 60606

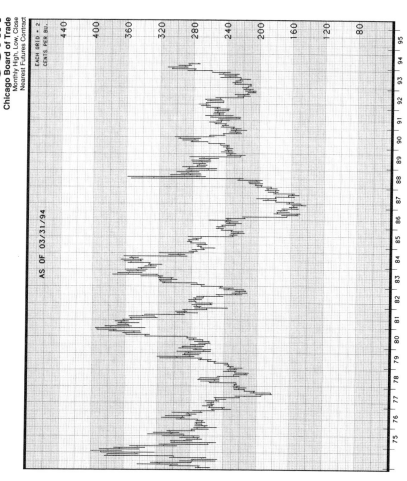

CORN
Chicago Board of Trade
Monthly High, Low, Close
Nearest Futures Contract

EACH GRID = 2
CENTS PER BU.

AS OF 03/31/94

CONTRACT SPECIFICATIONS

Exchange
Chicago Board of Trade

Trading Hours
9:30 a.m. to 1:15 p.m. Central Time

Trading Months
March, May, July, September and December

Contract Size
5,000 Bushels

Prices Quoted In
Cents per Bushel

Minimum Fluctuation
.25 cent

Value of Minimum Fluctuation
$12.50

Maximum Permissible Limit (variable limit)
12 cents

Value of Maximum Permissible Limit
$600

First Delivery Notice
Last business day of the month preceding delivery
month.

Last Trading Day
8th business day prior to the end of the month.

Crop Year
October 1 to September 30

10 Year Weekly Nearest Future
High: 366.00 (May '84 on 5-21-84)
Low: 142.00 (Mar '87 on 2-17-87)

20 Year Monthly Nearest Future
High: 400.00 (Dec '74 on 10-4-74)
Low: 133.13 (Dec '72 on 11-10-72)

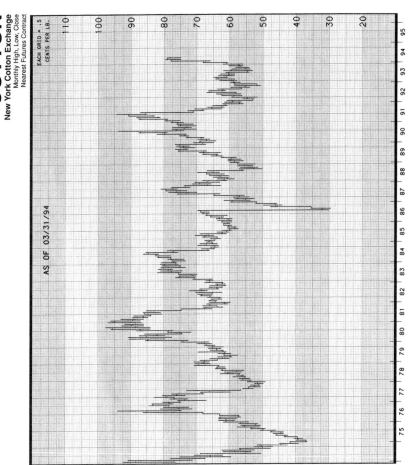

COTTON

New York Cotton Exchange
Monthly High, Low, Close
Nearest Futures Contract

EACH GRID = .5
CENTS PER LB.

AS OF 03/31/94

CONTRACT SPECIFICATIONS

Exchange
New York Cotton Exchange

Trading Hours
10:30 a.m. to 2:40 p.m. Eastern Time

Trading Months
March, May, July, October, and December

Contract Size
50,000 lbs.

Prices Quoted In
Cents per lb.

Minimum Fluctuation
.01 cent

Value of Minimum Fluctuation
$5.00

Maximum Permissible Limit
2 cents

Value of Maximum Permissible Limit
$1,000

First Delivery Notice
Five full business days prior to first business day of delivery month.

Last Trading Day
17th business day prior to the end of the month.

10 Year Weekly Nearest Future
High: 93.90 (Jul '90 on 7-5-90)
Low: 29.50 (Oct '86 on 8-6-86)

20 Year Monthly Nearest Future
High: 97.77 (Oct '80 on 9-12-80)
Low: 29.50 (Oct '86 on 8-6-86)

Reprinted with permission © 1994 Knight-Ridder Financial
30 South Wacker Drive, Suite 1820, Chicago, Illinois 60606

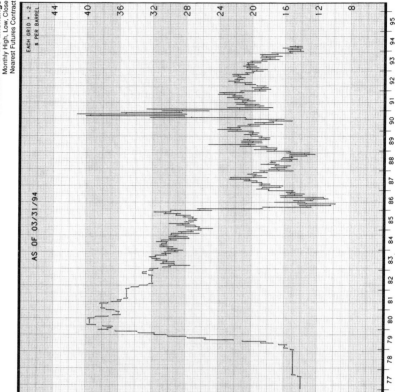

LIGHT

CRUDE OIL

New York Mercantile Exchange
Monthly High, Low, Close
Nearest Futures Contract

AS OF 03/31/94

EACH GRID = .2
$ PER BARREL

CONTRACT SPECIFICATIONS

Exchange
New York Mercantile Exchange

Trading Hours
5:00 p.m. to 8:00 a.m. (ACCESS)
9:45 a.m. to 3:10 p.m. Eastern Time

Trading Months
All months

Contract Size
1,000 barrels

Prices Quoted In
Dollars per barrel

Minimum Fluctuation
1 cent

Value of Minimum Fluctuation
$10.00

Maximum Permissible Limit (variable limit)
$1.00

Value of Maximum Permissible Limit
$1,000

First Delivery Notice
First business day of the contract month.

Last Trading Day
3rd business day preceding the 25th calendar day
of the month before the contract month.

10 Year Weekly Nearest Future
High: 41.15 (Nov 90) on 10-10-90)
Low: 9.75 (May 86 on 4-1-86)

20 Year Monthly Nearest Future
High: 41.15 (Nov 90 on 10-10-90)
Low: 9.75 (May 86 on 4-1-86)

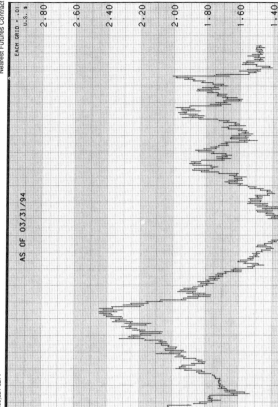

KNIGHT-RIDDER
FINANCIAL

30 South Wacker Drive, Suite 1820
Chicago, Illinois 60606-7498
(312)454-1801 (800)621-5271

BRITISH POUND

International Monetary Market
Monthly High, Low, Close
Nearest Futures Contract

AS OF 03/31/94

EACH GRID = .01
U.S. $

CONTRACT SPECIFICATIONS

Exchange
International Monetary Market Division of the Chicago Mercantile Exchange

Trading Hours
2:30 p.m. to 6:00 a.m (GLOBEX)
7:20 a.m. to 2:00 p.m. Central Time

Trading Months
March, June, September, and December

Contract Size
62,500 Pounds Sterling

Prices Quoted In
U.S. Dollars

Minimum Fluctuation
2 points ($.0002 per Pound Sterling)

Value of Minimum Fluctuation
$12.50

Maximum Permissible Limit
None

Delivery Days
Delivery shall be made on the 3rd Wednesday of the contract month. If that day is not a business day (in the country of delivery), delivery shall be made on the next business day immediately succeeding.

Last Trading Day
Futures trading shall terminate on the 2nd business day immediately preceding the delivery day of the contract month.

10 Year Weekly Nearest Future
High: 2.0088 (Sep '92 on 9-8-92)
Low: 1.0345 (Mar '85 on 2-26-85)

20 Year Monthly Nearest Future
High: 2.4485 (Dec '80 on 11-3-80)
Low: 1.0345 (Mar '85 on 2-26-85)

AUSTRALIAN DOLLAR
International Monetary Market
Monthly Nearest Futures

AS OF 05/31/94

EACH GRID = .005
US$ PER AD

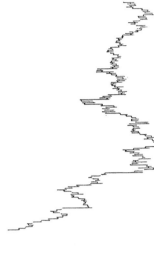

CONTRACT SPECIFICATIONS

Where traded
Chicago Mercantile Exchange (IMM)

Trading Hours (New York time)
8:20 am to 3:00 pm

Contract size
100,000 AD

How price is quoted
Dollars per AD

Minimum fluctuation Per 0.0001
$10.00

Value 100 point move
$1,000

Maximum trading limit from previous close
No limit

SWISS FRANC

International Monetary Market
Monthly High, Low, Close
Nearest Futures Contract

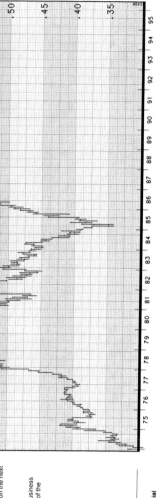

EACH GRID = .0025
U.S. $

AS OF 03/31/94

CONTRACT SPECIFICATIONS

Exchange
International Monetary Market Division of the Chicago
Mercantile Exchange

Trading Hours
2:30 p.m. to 6:00 a.m (GLOBEX)
7:20 a.m. to 2:00 p.m. Central Time

Trading Months
March, June, September, and December

Contract Size
125,000 Swiss Franc

Prices Quoted In
U.S. Dollars

Minimum Fluctuation
1 point ($.0001 per Swiss Franc)

Value of Minimum Fluctuation
$12.50

Maximum Permissible Limit
None

Delivery Days
Delivery shall be made on the 3rd Wednesday of the
contract month. If that day is not a business day (in the
country of delivery), delivery shall be made on the next
business day immediately succeeding.

Last Trading Day
Futures trading shall terminate on the 2nd business
day immediately preceding the delivery day of the
contract month.

10 Year Weekly Nearest Future
High: .8209 (Dec '92 on 10-5-92)
Low: .3408 (Mar '85 on 2-26-85)

20 Year Monthly Nearest Future
High: .8209 (Dec '92 on 10-5-92)
Low: .2908 (Mar '74 on 1-8-74)

DEUTSCHE MARK

International Monetary Market
Monthly High, Low, Close
Nearest Futures Contract

AS OF 03/31/94

EACH GRID = .0025   U.S. $

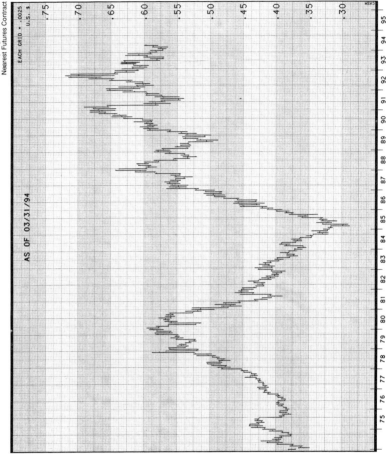

CONTRACT SPECIFICATIONS

Exchange
International Monetary Market Division of the Chicago Mercantile Exchange

Trading Hours
2:30 p.m. to 6:00 a.m. (GLOBEX)
7:20 a.m. to 2:00 p.m. Central Time

Trading Months
March, June, September, and December

Contract Size
125,000 Deutsche Mark

Prices Quoted In
U.S. Dollars

Minimum Fluctuation
1 point ($.0001 per Deutsche Mark)

Value of Minimum Fluctuation
$12.50

Maximum Permissible Limit
None

Delivery Days
Delivery shall be made on the 3rd Wednesday of the contract month. If that day is not a business day (in the country of delivery), delivery shall be made on the next business day immediately succeeding.

Last Trading Day
Futures trading shall terminate on the 2nd business day immediately preceding the delivery day of the contract month.

10 Year Weekly Nearest Future
High: .7196 (Sep '92 on 9-2-92)
Low: .2881 (Mar '85 on 2-26-85)

20 Year Monthly Nearest Future
High: .7196 (Sep '92 on 9-2-92)
Low: .2881 (Mar '85 on 2-26-85)

JAPANESE YEN
International Monetary Market
Monthly High, Low, Close
Nearest Futures Contract

EACH GRID = .005
U.S. CENTS

AS OF 03/31/94

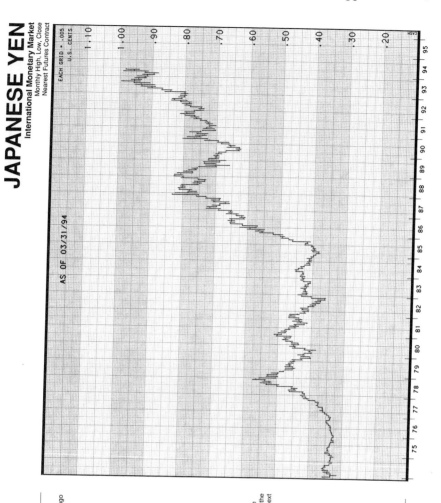

CONTRACT SPECIFICATIONS

Exchange
International Monetary Market Division of the Chicago
Mercantile Exchange

Trading Hours
2:30 p.m. to 6:00 a.m (GLOBEX)
7:20 a.m. to 2:00 p.m. Central Time

Trading Months
March, June, September, and December

Contract Size
12,500,000 Japanese Yen

Prices Quoted In
U.S. Cents

Minimum Fluctuation
1 point ($.0001 per)

Value of Minimum Fluctuation
$12.50

Maximum Permissible Limit
None

Delivery Days
Delivery shall be made on the 3rd Wednesday of the
contract month. If that day is not a business day (in the
country of delivery), delivery shall be made on the next
business day immediately succeeding.

Last Trading Day
Futures trading shall terminate on the 2nd business
day immediately preceding the delivery day of the
contract month.

10 Year Weekly Nearest Future
High: .9959 (Sep '93 on 8-17-93)
Low: .3794 (Mar '85 on 2-25-83)

20 Year Monthly Nearest Future
High: .9959 (Sep '93 on 8-17-93)
Low: .3130 (Mar '74 on 1-23-74)

NEW YORK
GOLD
Commodity Exchange, Inc.
Monthly High, Low, Close
Nearest Futures Contract

AS OF 03/31/94

EACH GRID = .5
$ PER TROY OZ.

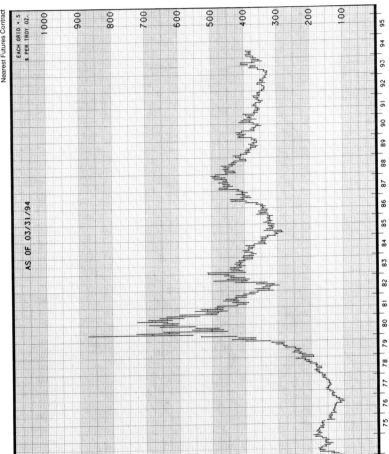

CONTRACT SPECIFICATIONS

Exchange
New York Commodity Exchange, Inc. (COMEX)

Trading Hours
8:20 a.m. to 2:30 p.m. Eastern Time

Trading Months
February, April, June, August, October, December, and spot month

Contract Size
100 troy ounces

Prices Quoted In
Dollars per troy ounce

Minimum Fluctuation
10 cents

Value of Minimum Fluctuation
$10.00

Maximum Permissible Limit
None

First Delivery Notice
First business day of delivery month.

Last Trading Day
The 3rd to the last business day of a maturing delivery month.

10 Year Weekly Nearest Future
High: 502.30 (Dec '87 on 12-14-87)
Low: 281.20 (Mar '85 on 2-25-85)

20 Year Monthly Nearest Future
High: 875.00 (Feb '80 on 1-21-80)
Low: 116.80 (Cash on 1-2-74)

Reprinted with permission © 1994 Knight-Ridder Financial
30 South Wacker Drive, Suite 1820, Chicago, Illinois 60606

#2 HEATING OIL

New York Mercantile Exchange
Monthly High, Low, Close
Nearest Futures Contract

AS OF 03/31/94

EACH GRID = .005
$ PER GALLON

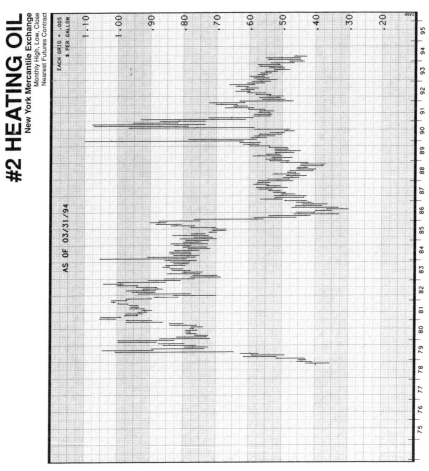

CONTRACT SPECIFICATIONS

Exchange
New York Mercantile Exchange

Trading Hours
5:00 p.m. to 8:00 a.m. (ACCESS)
9:50 a.m. to 3:10 p.m. Eastern Time

Trading Months
All months

Contract Size
42,000 gallons

Prices Quoted In
Cents per gallon

Minimum Fluctuation
.01 cent

Value of Minimum Fluctuation
$4.20

Maximum Permissible Limit (variable limit)
2 cents

Value of Maximum Permissible Limit
$840

First Delivery Notice
First business day of the contract month.

Last Trading Day
Last business day before the contract month.

10 Year Weekly Nearest Future
High: 1.10 (Jan '90 on 12-29-89)
Low: .2995 (Aug '86 on 7-14-86)

20 Year Monthly Nearest Future
High: 1.10 (Jan '90 on 12-29-89)
Low: .2995 (Aug '86 on 7-14-86)

Reprinted with permission © 1994 Knight-Ridder Financial
30 South Wacker Drive, Suite 1820, Chicago, Illinois 60606

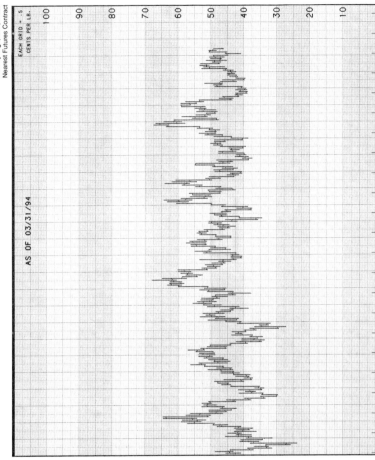

LIVE HOGS

Chicago Mercantile Exchange
Monthly High, Low, Close
Nearest Futures Contract

EACH GRID = .5
CENTS PER LB.

AS OF 03/31/94

CONTRACT SPECIFICATIONS

Exchange
Chicago Mercantile Exchange

Trading Hours
8:45 a.m. to 1:00 p.m. Central Time

Trading Months
February, April, June, July, August, October, and December

Contract Size
40,000 lb.

Prices Quoted In
Cents per lb

Minimum Fluctuation
.025 cent

Value of Minimum Fluctuation
$10.00

Maximum Permissible Limit
1-1/2 cents

Value of Maximum Permissible Limit
$600

First Delivery Notice
Delivery may be made on Monday, Tuesday, Wednesday, or Thursday after the 6th calendar day of the month.

Last Trading Day
Business day immediately preceding the last 5 business days of the contract month.

10 Year Weekly Nearest Future
High: 67.45 (Jun '90 on 5-29-90)
Low: 34.45 (Oct '85 on 9-9-85)

20 Year Monthly Nearest Future
High: 68.00 (Aug '82 on 8-20-82)
Low: 23.80 (Jun '74 on 6-11-74)

Reprinted with permission © 1994 Knight-Ridder Financial
30 South Wacker Drive, Suite 1820, Chicago, Illinois 60606

CONTRACT SPECIFICATIONS

Where traded
Chicago Mercantile Exchange

Trading Hours (New York time)
10:00 am to 2:05 pm

Contract size
160,000 board feet

How price is quoted
Dollars per 1,000 board feet

Minimum fluctuation Per 1,000 board feet
10 cents

Per contract
$16.00

Value $1.00 move
$160.00

Maximum trading limit from previous close
$5.00 per 1,000 board feet (equals $800)

Reprinted with permission © 1994 Knight-Ridder Financial
30 South Wacker Drive, Suite 1820, Chicago, Illinois 60606

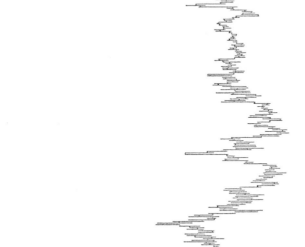

LUMBER
Chicago Mercantile Exchange
Monthly Nearest Futures

EACH GRID = 2
$ PER 1,000 BD FT

AS OF 05/31/94

CONTRACT SPECIFICATIONS

Where traded
New York Mercantile Exchange

Trading Hours (New York time)
8:20 am to 2:30 pm

Contract size
50 troy ounces

How price is quoted
Dollars per troy ounce

Minimum fluctuation: Per pound
10 cents

Per contract
$5.00

Value $1.00 move
$50.00

Maximum trading limit from previous close
$25.00

PLATINUM
New York Mercantile Exchange
Monthly Selected Futures

EACH GRID = 5
$ PER TROT OZ.

AS OF 05/31/94

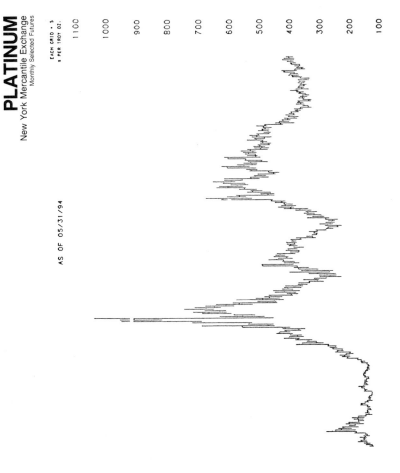

Reprinted with permission © 1994 Knight-Ridder Financial
30 South Wacker Drive, Suite 1820, Chicago, Illinois 60606

FROZEN
PORK BELLIES
Chicago Mercantile Exchange
Monthly High, Low, Close
Nearest Futures Contract

AS OF 03/31/94

EACH GRID = .5
CENTS PER LB.

CONTRACT SPECIFICATIONS

Exchange
Chicago Mercantile Exchange

Trading Hours
8:45 a.m. to 1:00 p.m. Central Time

Trading Months
February, March, May, July, August

Contract Size
40,000 lb.

Prices Quoted In
Cents per lb.

Minimum Fluctuation
.025 cent

Value of Minimum Fluctuation
$10.00

Maximum Permissible Limit
2 cents

Value of Maximum Permissible Limit
$800

First Delivery Notice
First business day of contract month.

Last Trading Day
Business day immediately preceding the last 5 business days of the contract month.

10 Year Weekly Nearest Future
High: 92.50 (Aug '87 on 8-7-87)
Low: 24.27 (Aug '89 on 8-1-89)

20 Year Monthly Nearest Future
High: 105.10 (Aug '75 on 8-14-75)
Low: 24.27 (Aug '89 on 8-1-89)

Reprinted with permission © 1994 Knight-Ridder Financial
30 South Wacker Drive, Suite 1820, Chicago, Illinois 60606

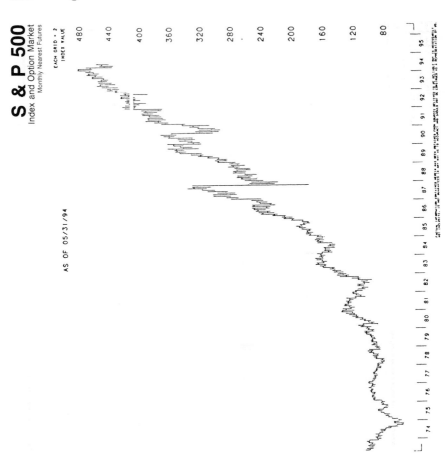

S & P 500
Index and Option Market
Monthly Nearest Futures

EACH GRID = 2
INDEX VALUE

AS OF 05/31/94

CONTRACT SPECIFICATIONS

Where traded
Chicago Mercantile Exchange (IOM)

Trading Hours (New York time)
9:30 am to 4:15 pm

Contract size
$500 × index

How price is quoted
Index

Minimum fluctuation Per .05
$25.00

Value 100 point move
$500.00

Maximum trading limit from previous close
None

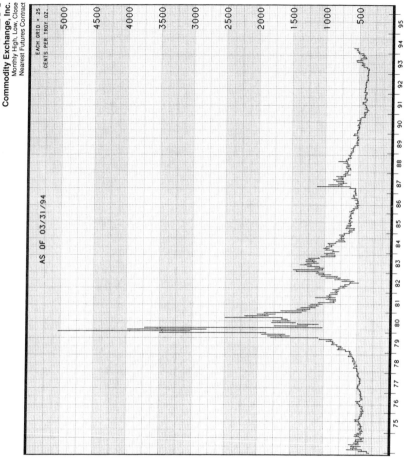

NEW YORK
SILVER
Commodity Exchange, Inc.
Monthly High, Low, Close
Nearest Futures Contract

EACH GRID = 25
CENTS PER TROY OZ.

AS OF 03/31/94

CONTRACT SPECIFICATIONS

Exchange
New York Commodity Exchange, Inc. (COMEX)

Trading Hours
8:25 a.m. to 2:25 p.m. Eastern Time

Trading Months
March, May, July, September, December
and spot month

Contract Size
5,000 troy ounces

Prices Quoted In
Cents per troy ounce

Minimum Fluctuation
.10 cents

Value of Minimum Fluctuation
$5.00

Maximum Permissible Limit
None

First Delivery Notice
Last business day of calendar month preceding
month of delivery.

Last Trading Day
The 3rd to the last business day of a maturing delivery
month.

10 Year Weekly Nearest Future
High: 1,125.00 (Apr '87 on 4-27-87)
Low: 350.80 (Feb '91 on 2-22-91)

20 Year Monthly Nearest Future
High: 5,036.00 (Jan '80 on 1-18-80)
Low: 323.50 (Jan '74 on 1-4-74)

Reprinted with permission © 1994 Knight-Ridder Financial
30 South Wacker Drive, Suite 1820, Chicago, Illinois 60606

SOYBEANS

Chicago Board of Trade
Monthly High, Low, Close
Nearest Futures Contract

AS OF 03/31/94

EACH GRID = 5
CENTS PER BU.

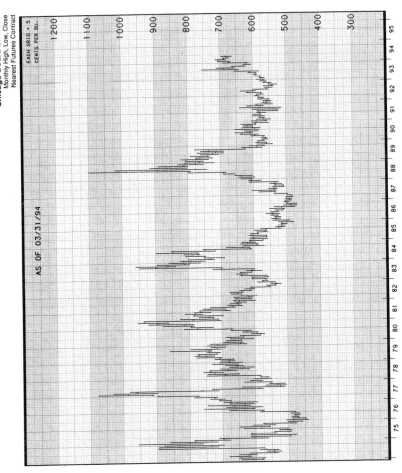

CONTRACT SPECIFICATIONS

Exchange
Chicago Board of Trade

Trading Hours
9:30 a.m. to 1:15 p.m. Central Time

Trading Months
January, March, May, July, August, September and November

Contract Size
5,000 Bushels

Prices Quoted In
Cents per Bushel

Minimum Fluctuation
.25 cent

Value of Minimum Fluctuation
$12.50

Maximum Permissible Limit (variable limit)
30 cents

Value of Maximum Permissible Limit
$1,500

First Delivery Notice
Last business day of the month preceding delivery month.

Last Trading Day
8th business day prior to the end of the month.

Crop Year
September 1 to August 30

10 Year Weekly Nearest Future
High: 1,099.50 (Jul '88 on 6-23-88)
Low: 467.50 (Sep '86 on 9-2-86)

20 Year Monthly Nearest Future
High: 1,099.50 (Jul '88 on 6-23-88)
Low: 439.50 (Jan '76 on 12-15-76)

Reprinted with permission © 1994 Knight-Ridder Financial
30 South Wacker Drive, Suite 1820, Chicago, Illinois 60606

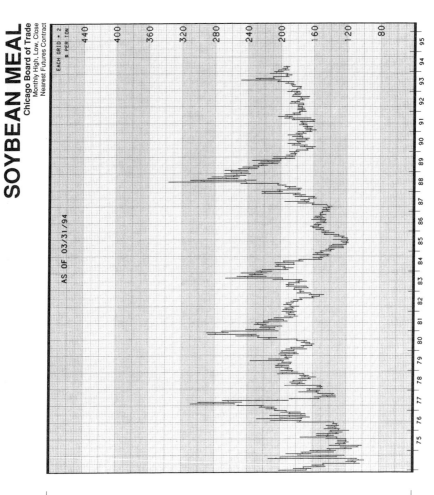

SOYBEAN MEAL

Chicago Board of Trade
Monthly High, Low, Close
Nearest Futures Contract

AS OF 03/31/94

EACH GRID = 2
$ PER TON

CONTRACT SPECIFICATIONS

Exchange
Chicago Board of Trade

Trading Hours
9:30 a.m. to 1:15 p.m. Central Time

Trading Months
January, March, May, July, August, September,
October and December

Contract Size
100 short tons (2,000 lbs. per ton)

Prices Quoted In
Dollars per ton

Minimum Fluctuation
10 cents

Value of Minimum Fluctuation
$10.00

Maximum Permissible Limit (variable limit)
$10.00

Value of Maximum Permissible Limit
$1,000

First Delivery Notice
Last business day of the month preceding delivery
month.

Last Trading Day
8th business day prior to the end of the month.

Crop Year
October 1 to September 30

10 Year Weekly Nearest Future
High: 336.50 (Jul '88 on 6-23-88)
Low: 117.50 (Jul '85 on 7-1-85)

20 Year Monthly Nearest Future
High: 336.50 (Jul '88 on 6-23-88)
Low: 97.76 (Jul '74 on 6-19-74)

Reprinted with permission © 1994 Knight-Ridder Financial
30 South Wacker Drive, Suite 1820, Chicago, Illinois 60606

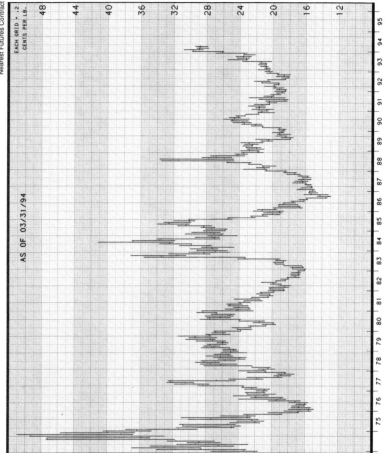

SOYBEAN OIL

Chicago Board of Trade
Monthly High, Low, Close
Nearest Futures Contract

AS OF 03/31/94

EACH GRID = .2
CENTS PER LB.

CONTRACT SPECIFICATIONS

Exchange
Chicago Board of Trade

Trading Hours
9:30 a.m. to 1:15 p.m. Central Time

Trading Months
January, March, May, July, August, September,
October and December

Contract Size
60,000 lbs.

Prices Quoted In
Cents per lb.

Minimum Fluctuation
.01 cent

Value of Minimum Fluctuation
$6.00

Maximum Permissible Limit (variable limit)
1 cent

Value of Maximum Permissible Limit
$600

First Delivery Notice
Last business day of the month preceding delivery
month.

Last Trading Day
8th business day prior to the end of the month.

Crop Year
October 1 to September 30

10 Year Weekly Nearest Future
High: 41.15 (May '84 on 5-18-84)
Low: 12.95 (Sep '86 on 9-2-86)

20 Year Monthly Nearest Future
High: 51.00 (Oct 74 on 10-1-74)
Low: 12.95 (Sep '86 on 9-2-86)

Reprinted with permission © 1994 Knight-Ridder Financial
30 South Wacker Drive, Suite 1820, Chicago, Illinois 60606

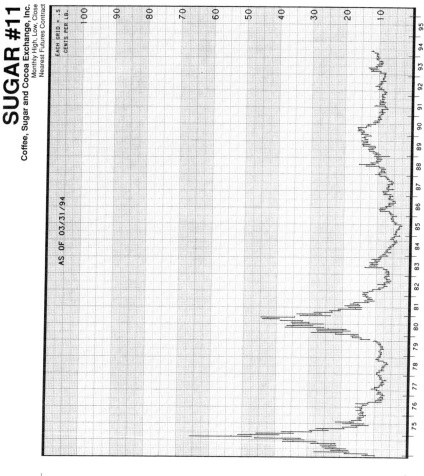

SUGAR #11

Coffee, Sugar and Cocoa Exchange, Inc.

Monthly High, Low, Close
Nearest Futures Contract

AS OF 03/31/94

EACH GRID = .5
CENTS PER LB.

CONTRACT SPECIFICATIONS

Exchange
New York Coffee, Sugar and Cocoa Exchange

Trading Hours
10:00 a.m. to 1:43 p.m. Eastern Time

Trading Months
March, May, July and October

Contract Size
112,000 lb.

Prices Quoted In
Cents per lb.

Minimum Fluctuation
.01 cent

Value of Minimum Fluctuation
$11.20

Maximum Permissible Limit (variable limit)
.50 cent

Value of Maximum Permissible Limit
$560

First Delivery Notice
First business day of the delivery month.

Last Trading Day
Last business day of month preceding delivery month.

Crop Year
October 1 to September 30

10 Year Weekly Nearest Future
High: 16.28 (May '90 on 3-16-90)
Low: 2.30 (Jul '85 on 6-28-85)

20 Year Monthly Nearest Future
High: 66.00 (Mar '75 on 11-21-74)
Low: 2.30 (Jul '85 on 6-28-85)

Reprinted with permission © 1994 Knight-Ridder Financial
30 South Wacker Drive, Suite 1820, Chicago, Illinois 60606

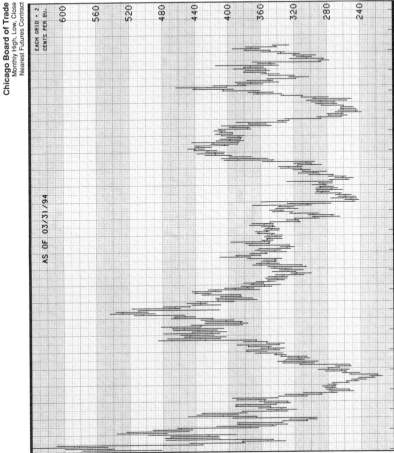

WHEAT

Chicago Board of Trade
Monthly High, Low, Close
Nearest Futures Contract

EACH GRID = 2
CENTS PER BU.

AS OF 03/31/94

CONTRACT SPECIFICATIONS

Exchange
Chicago Board of Trade

Trading Hours
9:30 a.m. to 1:15 p.m. Central Time

Trading Months
March, May, July, September, and December

Contract Size
5,000 bushels

Prices Quoted In
Cents per bushel

Minimum Fluctuation
.25 cent

Value of Minimum Fluctuation
$12.50

Maximum Permissible Limit (variable limit)
20 cents

Value of Maximum Permissible Limit
$1,000

First Delivery Notice
Last business day of the month preceding delivery month.

Last Trading Day
8th business day prior to the end of the month.

Crop Year
July 1 to June 30

10 Year Weekly Nearest Future
High: 463.25 (Mar '92 on 2-10-92)
Low: 238.00 (Dec '90 on 11-29-90)

20 Year Monthly Nearest Future
High: 645.00 (Mar '74 on 2-26-74)
Low: 214.25 (Sep '77 on 8-22-77)

3-Month
EURODOLLARS
International Monetary Market
Monthly High, Low, Close
Nearest Futures Contract

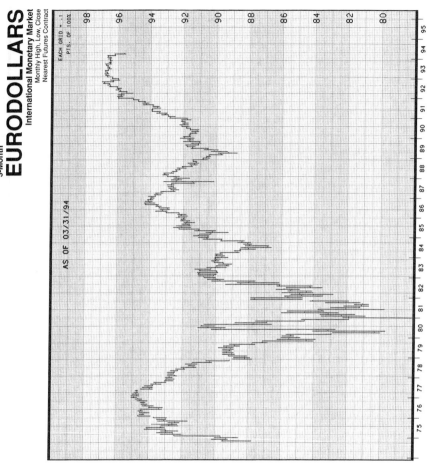

AS OF 03/31/94

EACH GRID = .1
PTS. OF 100%

CONTRACT SPECIFICATIONS

Exchange
International Monetary Market Division of the Chicago Mercantile Exchange

Trading Hours
3:00 p.m. to 6:00 a.m (GLOBEX)
7:20 a.m. to 2:00 p.m. Central Time

Trading Months
March, June, September, and December

Contract Size
$1,000,000

Prices Quoted In
Prices quoted in terms of IMM index. Index is based on the difference between actual Eurodollar Yield and 100.00. Eurodollar Yield of 6.00 percent would be quoted on the IMM at 94.00

Minimum Fluctuation
1 point (.01 of 1.00 percent)

Value of Minimum Fluctuation
$25.00

Maximum Permissible Limit
None

Delivery Day
Last day of trading.

Last Trading Day
Futures trading shall terminate on the 2nd (London) business day before the 3rd Wednesday of the contract month.

10 Year Weekly Nearest Future
High: 97.01 (Dec '92 on 10-1-92)
Low: 86.63 (Sep '84 on 6-22-84)

20 Year Monthly Nearest Future
High: 97.01 (Dec '92 on 10-1-92)
Low: 77.94 (Cash on 12-19-80)

Reprinted with permission © 1994 Knight-Ridder Financial
30 South Wacker Drive, Suite 1820, Chicago, Illinois 60606

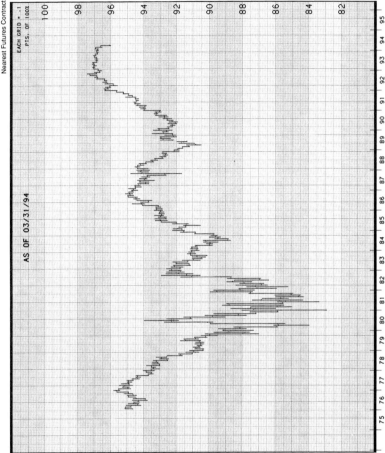

3-Month
U.S. T-BILLS
International Monetary Market
Monthly High, Low, Close
Nearest Futures Contract

AS OF 03/31/94

EACH GRID = .1
PTS. OF 100%

CONTRACT SPECIFICATIONS

Exchange
International Monetary Market Division of the Chicago Mercantile Exchange

Trading Hours
3:00 p.m. to 6:00 a.m (GLOBEX),
7:20 a.m. to 2:00 p.m. CT

Trading Months
March, June, September, and December

Contract Size
$1,000,000

Prices Quoted In
Prices quoted in terms of IMM index. Index is based on the difference between actual T-Bill Yield and 100.00. T-Bill Yield of 6.00 percent would be quoted on the IMM at 94.00

Minimum Fluctuation
1 point (.01 of 1.00 percent)

Value of Minimum Fluctuation
$25.00

Maximum Permissible Limit
None

Delivery Day
Delivery is on any of the 3 successive business days following the last trading day. The first delivery day is the first day of the spot month on which a 13-week T-Bill is issued and a one-year T-Bill has 13 weeks remaining to maturity.

Last Trading Day
Trading terminates on the business day immediately preceding first delivery day.

10 Year Weekly Nearest Future
High: 97.44 (Dec '92 on 10-5-92)
Low: 88.69 (Sep '84 on 6-11-84)

20 Year Monthly Nearest Future
High: 97.44 (Dec '92 on 10-5-92)
Low: 82.90 (Dec '80 on 12-11-80)

U.S. T-BONDS

Chicago Board of Trade
Monthly High, Low, Close
Nearest Futures Contract

EACH GRID = 16/32
PTS = 32NDS OF 100%

AS OF 03/31/94

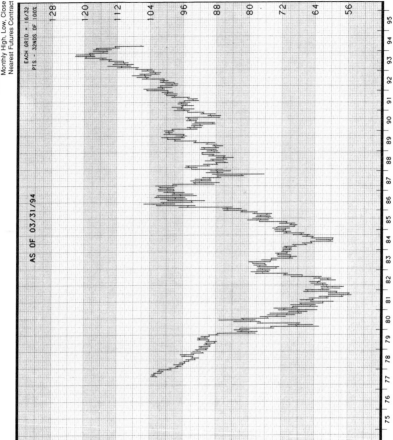

CONTRACT SPECIFICATIONS

Exchange
Chicago Board of Trade

Trading Hours
10:30 p.m. to 6:00 a.m. (GLOBEX)
5:20 p.m. to 8:05 p.m. / 7:20 a.m. to 2:00 p.m. CST
6:20 p.m. to 9:05 p.m. / 7:20 a.m. to 2:00 p.m. CDT

Trading Months
March, June, September, and December

Contract Size
U.S. Treasury Notes with $100,000 face value

Prices Quoted In
Points/32nd of 100%

Minimum Fluctuation
1/32

Value of Minimum Fluctuation
$31.25

Maximum Permissible Limit
96/32 or 3 points

Value of Maximum Permissible Limit
$3,000

First Delivery Notice
Last business day of the month preceding delivery.

Last Trading Day
8th business day prior to the end of the month.

10 Year Weekly Nearest Future
High: 122-10 (Sep '93 on 9-7-93)
Low: 59-12 (Sep '84 on 7-2-84)

20 Year Monthly Nearest Future
High: 122-10 (Sep '93 on 9-7-93)
Low: 55-08 (Dec '81 on 9-28-81)

10-Year
U.S. T-NOTES
Chicago Board of Trade
Monthly High, Low, Close
Nearest Futures Contract

AS OF 03/31/94

EACH GRID = 16/32
PTS - 32NDS OF 100%

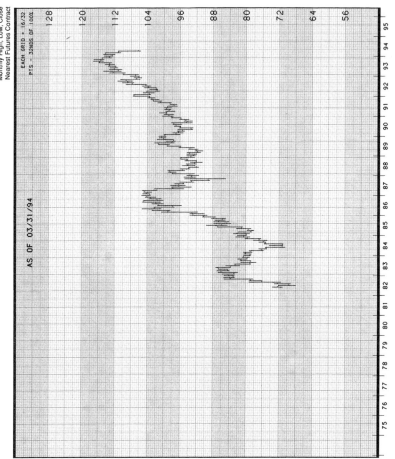

CONTRACT SPECIFICATIONS

Exchange
Chicago Board of Trade

Trading Hours
10:30 p.m. to 6:00 a.m. (GLOBEX)
5:20 p.m. to 8:05 p.m. / 7:20 a.m. to 2:00 p.m. CST
6:20 p.m. to 9:05 p.m. / 7:20 a.m. to 2:00 p.m. CDT

Trading Months
March, June, September, and December

Contract Size
U.S. Treasury Notes with $100,000 face value

Prices Quoted In
Points/32nd of 100%

Minimum Fluctuation
1/32

Value of Minimum Fluctuation
$31.25

Maximum Permissible Limit
96/32 or 3 points

Value of Maximum Permissible Limit
$3,000

First Delivery Notice
Last business day prior to the end of the month.

Last Trading Day
8th business day prior to the end of the month.

10 Year Weekly Nearest Future
High: 117-09 (Sep '93 on 9-7-93)
Low: 70-17 (Jun '84 on 5-30-84)

20 Year Monthly Nearest Future
High: 117-09 (Sep '93 on 9-7-93)
Low: 68-01 (Sep '82 on 6-23-82)

HANG SENG INDEX
Hong Kong Futures Exchange
Monthly Nearest Futures

AS OF 05/31/94

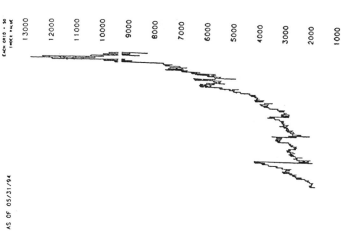

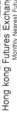

CONTRACT SPECIFICATIONS

Where traded
Hong Kong Futures Exchange

Trading Hours (Hong Kong time)
10:00 to 12:30 and 2:30 to 3:45

Contract size
HK $50 × Index

How price is quoted
Index

Minimum fluctuation: Per 1 point
HK $50

Value 100 point move
HK $5,000 (US $650)

Maximum trading limit
500 points per trading session above or below

from previous close
the last closing quotation. No limit spot month.

Reprinted with permission © 1994 Knight-Ridder Financial
30 South Wacker Drive, Suite 1820, Chicago, Illinois 60606

CONTRACT SPECIFICATIONS

Where traded
Singapore Int'l Monetary Exchange (SIMEX)

Trading Hours
08:00 — 11:15

Singapore time
12:15 — 19:05

Contract size
JPY 100,000,000

How price is quoted
Japanese Yen

Minimum fluctuation Per 0.01%
JPY 2,500

Maximum trading limit from previous close
No limit

3-MONTH EUROYEN
Singapore Int'l Monetary Exchange
Monthly nearest Futures

AS OF 05/31/94

EACH GRID = .05
PTS. OF 100%

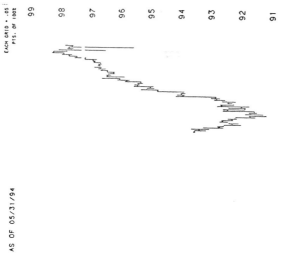

Reprinted with permission © 1994 Knight-Ridder Financial
30 South Wacker Drive, Suite 1820, Chicago, Illinois 60606

JAPANESE 10-YEAR BOND

SIMEX
Monthly Nearest Futures

AS OF 05/31/94

CONTRACT SPECIFICATIONS

Where traded
Singapore International Monetary Exchange
(SIMEX)

Trading Hours
07:45 — 10:30

(Singapore time)
11:30 — 17:00

Contract size
JPY 50,000,000

How price is quoted
Per 100 JPY face value

Minimum fluctuation: Per contract
0.01 JPY per 100 JPY face value
= JPY 5,000 per tick

Maximum trading limit from previous close
No limit

NIKKEI
SIMEX
Monthly Nearest Futures

AS OF 05/31/94

EACH GRID = 2
INDEX VALUE

CONTRACT SPECIFICATIONS

Where traded
Singapore International Monetary Exchange
(SIMEX)

Trading Hours
08:00 — 10:15

(Singapore time)
11:15 — 2:15

Contract size
JPY 500 × Index

How price is quoted
Index

Minimum fluctuation Per 5 point
JPY 2,500

Value 100 point move
JPY 50,000

Maximum trading limit from previous close
5% from previous close; stop trading for 15
minutes. Then, 10% from previous close;
stop trading for 15 minutes more.

Index

Australian dollar, trends 112

bad markets 41–4
bail out point 53
Barker 80
bear markets
  entrenched, buying against 7
  see also selling
best bets trading 31–5
  Hite on 70–1
Bollinger bands in technical trading
    system 76
Bouriene 11
brokerage advisories 14
bucket shops 1
bull markets
  entrenched, selling against 7
  see also buying
buying
  order entry procedures for 84
  strengths 63–8
  on weakness into support x

cattle (live) trends 104
China
  commodity exchanges 97
  forward markets 97
  futures markets 97, 101–2
  investment opportunities 95–9
cocoa trends 105
coffee trends 106
Commodity Research Bureau (CRB)
    22
Commodity speculation
  China 97
  order entry procedures for 84
  strategy for 6
composite decision 12

copper market
  long-term position on 27
  trends 107
corn market
  selling weakness 65
  spread chart 67
  trends 65, 108
cotton market
  long position on 48–9
  trends 49, 109
crude oil trends 110

day trader 27
Deng Xiaoping 95–6
derivatives, speculating on 11
desire to win 14–5
Deutsche mark, trends 114
Dies, Edward J. 2
Directional Movement Index 74–5
discipline 51–3
downtrending
  mixed strategy for 60–1
  strategy for 6, 7, 8
  trading in 33, 74–5

entry to market
  signals 32
  in uptrend 34
Eurodollars trends 129
Euroyen (3-month) trends 134
exit from market
  signals 32
  in uptrend 34
exiting positions 8–9

fear of losing 14–5
forward markets, China 97
fundamental analysis 17

futures
  China, markets   97, 101–2
  in grain   22–3
  Hang Seng Index on   19–21
  markets, good and bad   41
  order entry procedures for   84
  predictions on   12
  price inversion in   66
  risk control   52

gap opening on high volume   6
gearing   ix
  high, in grain markets   66
gold trends   116
gossip and tips   37–40
grain futures   22–3

Hang Seng Index (Hong Kong)
  19–21
  daily chart   57
  trends   133
heating oil
  market   18–20
  trends   117
high leverage   5
Hite, Larry   31, 69–72
Hochheimer, Frank   80
hogs (live) trends   118
Hong Kong, investment opportunities
  98–9

IBM   38–9
information and technical analysis
  37–40
investment strategy
  importance of   5–9
  and Sun Tzu   25–9
Japanese 10-year bond, trends   135
Japanese yen, trends   115

Karr, Alphonse   3
keep it simple (KIS) approach to
  technical analysis   74, 79

leverage   ix
limit orders, procedures for   85
Livermore, Jesse Lauriston   1–4, 25
  on exiting trending positions   34
  on long positions   28–9, 48–50
long positions
  and bad markets   42
  on copper   27
  in Hang Seng Index   21
  perception versus reality   46–7
  predictions on   11–12
  trading   6
long shot trading   31–2
long-term trading   55–61

moving average systems in   81–2
  and short-term   59–61
losses   3
  avoiding   53
  confidence   73
  fear of   14–15
  and margin calls   64
  marked to the market   64
  by speculators   11–15
lumber trends   119

maintenance margin calls   63
margins
  calls, strategy for   63
  and risk control   52–3
market action versus market news
  37–40
market if touched order, procedures for
  86
market news versus market action
  37–40
markets
  good versus bad   41–4
  predictions   11–12
measured reactions to trends   6
Medbury, James K.   77
moving averages
  in mixed strategy   59
  as technical indicators   74, 79
Murphy's Law   x
  order entry procedures   88

new business margin calls   63
NIKKEI   32–3
  tradings   43
  trends   136
north moving markets   39

one cancels the other order, procedures
  for   86
on-line short-term chart
  presentations   2
on-line tick data   4
open interest, in technical analysis   17
options
  speculating on   11
  strategies   51
order entry procedures   83–9
  cancelling   87
  errors   87
  Murphy's Law   88
  trends and prices   88
overhead resistance   6–7
overtrading   52–3

paper portfolios   15
Patten, Chris   21
perception versus reality   45–50

pick off tops or bottoms   22, 55
pit gossip   40
platinum trends   120
pork bellies trends   121
portfolios, paper versus real time   15
position trader   27
pound stirling, trends   111
Precious Metals Index   24
price inversion in futures markets   66
protective stops   x
pyramiding   8, 64

real time portfolios   15
reality versus perception   45–50
recent reaction bottom   7
red ink, spilling   7
relative strength index (rsi) in technical
     trading system   76–7
reversal points in directional indicators
     75
risk control   51–3
   Hite on   71–2
   and margin calls   64
Runyon, Damon   31

scalp in large volume   5
selling
   order entry procedures for   84
   weaknesses   63–8
short interest, in technical analysis   17
short positions
   and bad markets   42
   perception versus reality   45–6
short-term scalping   51
short-term trading   55–61
   increasing focus on   55–7
   and long-term   59–61
   moving average systems in   82
sideways trends   6, 8
   trading in   33
silver trends   123
simple moving averages in trading
     strategy   32–3, 79
Singapore International Monetary
     Exchange (SIMEX)   32–3, 43
south moving markets   42
soybean trends   124
   meal   125
   oil   126
speculation
   losing money on   11–15
   on predictions   11–12
spot markets, and price inversions   66
spread margins   64, 67
spread order, procedures for   87
Standard & Poor 500, trends   122
Stochastics in technical trading system
     75–6

stock speculation, strategy for   6
stop orders, procedures for   85
stopped out   8, 34
straddle margins   64, 67
sugar
   long-term trading in   56
   market, news versus action   38–9
   trends   127
Sun Tzu   25–9
Swiss franc, trends   113

Taoism   25
technical analysis   17–24
   and tips and gossip   37–40
technical trading system   73–8
   moving average systems   79–82
tick-by-tick   2
   computerized chart   56
tips and gossip   37–40
trading
   strategy for   91–3
   trend following   32, 34
trends
   commodities *see* Appendix
   good and bad markets   43–4
   scalping against   8
   trading against   32
   trading with   32, 34
   see also downtrending; sideways
     trends; uptrending
triple top formations   56–7
Twain, Mark   43

United States T-Bills   92
   trends   130
United States T-Bonds, trends   58,
     131
United States T-Notes, trends   132
unwinding a spread position   68
uptrending
   of Hang Seng Index   21
   in heating oil market   18–20
   mixed strategy for   60–1
   strategy for   6, 7
   trading in   32–3, 74–5

Watts, Dickson   9
weighted moving averages in trading
     strategy   79
wheat markets
   buying strengths   65–6
   spread chart   67
   trends   66, 128
when done order, procedures for   86
wipe-outs   5

Yamani, Sheikh   18, 19